BODY ASCENSION SERIES BOOK ONE:

# AVATAR ANATOMY
## ~ *A Soul's Journey into the Body*

*Angela Ditch*

# Acknowledgements

I wish to thank all my teachers. Your willingness to step in service of others to share your gifts of knowledge, while holding the space for growth and transformation, has not only given me valuable tools, it has inspired me to the depths of my soul. Thank you!

The actual act of writing this first book has been an incredible journey and one in which two souls played a tremendous role.

*Lorinne*, one of my beautiful sisters and best friends, your unwavering confidence and belief in me and my path has been a lighthouse that illuminates all that is possible. Words cannot express the gratitude and love I have for you. You are an immense gift in my life. Thank you!

*Tom*, you are the most dynamic intuitive literary midwife. I can't imagine that anyone could have said more perfect things to me at such precise moments. Your coaching method and example would have been enough, but your matter-of-fact belief in me made me certain I could do this. Thank you!

# Introduction

Welcome to the *Body Ascension Series.*

Have you ever been to the optometrist? If you have you will remember the little machine that sits in front of your eyes while the doctor flips lenses, one at a time, in front of your view, with the simple question, "Better or worse?"

Some of the lenses bring clarity and some blur your vision. The goal of the appointment is find the right combination of lenses to allow YOU to see most clearly. YOU are unique. Others may have similar prescriptions but only you see the way you do.

*Body Ascension,* like all bodies of information, is a lens. It is a compilation of various teachings interpreted through the filter of my own experiences. I invite you to look through this lens and see how it feels to you. Please receive anything that brings you clarity and disregard anything that does not. For in the end we must all bow to our own true teacher, the one within.

### *"Ong Namo Guru Dev Namo"*
~ I bow to the divine teacher within

# Chapter 1

The day was sunny. It was June 22, the time of the summer solstice in Northern Alberta. A sense of hope and renewal filled the air as crops and gardens emerged from the soil and showed signs of great potential for the coming harvest. The warmth of the sun was at its peak as people breathed it in and shed more clothes to feel the heightened sense of the season. In Grande Prairie, Alberta, Canada, summer was savored for days like these.

My left arm leaned out of the open window of my Chevy S-10 truck. I was roaming the country roads of Grande Prairie, delivering rural route mail. My husband and I operated a transport business, and our primary contract was with the post office. It was one of the many ventures we had undertaken together.

Both of us, born Taurus, were natural manifesters, steeping in ambition. We continuously multiplied our business each year. In addition to already working seven days a week, we had just added a small farm to our plate. We acquired it mostly for the lifestyle it afforded, but also for the adventure of growing organic crops and developing new sources of income.

It was all very exciting, having been dreamed of, imagined, and discussed at great length, to then manifest through a magical series of synchronicities that typically guided our lives.

This was also a time of deep reflection, initiated by the overworked state of our bodies. Our minds were taxed in every moment, as the work seemed to never cease or pause. We were masters at what we did, but simply did too much, and the continuous states of high-stress hormones running through our bodies affected every aspect of our beings.

As a couple, we had many dysfunctional challenges in our relationship that were amplified by these states of high stress and then avoided by the lack of time to face them. To top things off, the price of everything had just escalated and the flow of money going out was gaining on the flow of money coming in. I had become a master juggler of resources to keep us rolling, but the exhaustion of the track we were on was starting to catch us both.

For several weeks prior to this day, I would drive along the country roads and ponder the point of life and the point of living. This was not in a suicidal way, but more in a "What for?" kind of way. I was depressed. The road ahead of me appeared tiring and our relationship was very strained. To add to that, my mother- and father-in-law were living with us as they sought the perfect home to relocate back in our area.

My mother- and father-in-law were beautiful people whose only intent was to assist us in any way they could, and I loved them both dearly. It was simply that with all of the stresses in my life, I was overwhelmed and no longer felt that I could just unplug at the end of the day with their presence in my house.

As I wandered around the rural routes in full contemplation of this point of living, I began to fantasize about what it would be like to die. I wasn't preoccupied with the how or why, but the funeral itself. Each day, this escalated, and I found myself becoming more deeply entrenched in it. I wanted to be less like this, but somehow, the fascination with the scene of my funeral sucked me deeper into a hole of morbid self-pity. The very essence of this dark state of mind permeated the core of me and echoed in every thought and emotion. I was in a mild form of depression.

As I curved around these roads each day, I found a sense of peace and calm in the fantasy of my funeral. Who would come? What would they say about me? Would they miss me as much as I would expect, and how would my partner be? Would he be devastated and wish he could bring me back, or feel a sense of relief that an easy way out had been found, or maybe both?

All of these questions began to swirl. I even started to imagine the music, and then assembled it onto a cassette tape to listen to over and over again. I would sing the songs and imagine the tears that would fall as these profound musical scores would touch people's hearts on such a sad occasion. Such a young woman, twenty-four years old, gone from the earth. It was very dramatic. I was totally immersed in self-pity and I was completely trapped in it.

This particular day, June 22, was the day of the big farm machinery auction. We had just purchased our farmland, and my partner was off choosing the best options of equipment, and I was covering two rural routes that day. I loved these routes. I'd spend many hours driving around the countryside, in all kinds of weather and road conditions, meeting the most wonderful farmers and souls who absolutely embodied the lifestyle of country living and farming. These were hardworking, salt-of-the-earth types, who had faced many challenges and had a deep and honoring respect for Mother Nature and the uncontrollable results that come from her whims and changing flows.

On this particular day, I had begun on the west side of town, on Rural Route 2, and was now beginning my approach onto Rural Route 1 on the east side. Driving around the same circles each day was repetitive, and one way to make that more interesting was to race one's best time. I had something I wanted to do at the end of my deliveries that day, so this day would need to be my most efficient. This was my prime objective. I was invigorated to see how I would do when I put all of my focus to the task.

I was coming up on a main artery, and a set of railway tracks just beyond it, when I saw the train heading for the intersection. It was a long parade of railcars and I knew that if I did not pass first, I would be stuck for many minutes while it held me back from my flow.

I looked both ways for oncoming traffic and accelerated. When you drive these roads day after day in every condition, you get really good at judging the distances and the openings they present. I was exceptionally good at this. I could easily see that I had plenty of room to make the crossing of both the road and the tracks, so I pushed the gas pedal to the floor.

I flew over the tracks to the sound of the train horn blasting, and a few seconds later, the train crossed the intersection. I was off to the next group of mailboxes.

As I drove, the little voice in my head began to speak. *"You never know what might come along to stop you from something much worse,"* it began. I screwed up my face like a teenager refusing to acknowledge adult logic and continued on.

This little voice popped in and out of my head throughout my whole life, usually giving me random bits of information that were relatively unimportant in the big scheme of life, like reminders in the grocery store or warnings when I would be about to lose something. Sometimes, the voice would work to my advantage and seem otherworldly, completely magical and intuitive. But as soon as I would try to capitalize on that, it would disappear.

I recall one summer, as a young girl, playing cards at the kitchen table in our house. My grandmother, my two aunts, and my mother were all in the game. All of the women were busy visiting and telling stories about this person and that gathering, and this issue and that calamity. Their conversation was pleasant but a bit of a blur for me. My mind was zoning out; the little voice was talking softly in my ear.

My full attention was on the cards. I liked to win. Okay, I loved to win. It seemed that I was able to see ten steps ahead of what would happen and what would be played, which cards I would need in exact suits and timing. The conversation flowed, the cards got played, and moment after moment, I was cleaning up the table with my lucky streak. At first, it went unnoticed, as the conversation was captivating the players and no one was attached to the score, but then it started to become an unusual pattern and everyone became quiet.

I needed a jack, one appeared. I needed a heart, one appeared. Everything was happening so automatically that I no longer even thought about another possibility. It just was what it was, perfectly orchestrated, as the little voice stated the next requirement softly in my ear. Ten of hearts—yes; king of diamonds—yes; and so on. As though by simply placing my right hand over the deck and knowing the card required, it brought it magically to the surface of the cut. Mind over cards, I called it. It was so easy. Nobody liked to play cards with me in those days.

Meanwhile, back on the rural route, it seemed that there were extra obstacles to face all along the way that day, but I maneuvered around them and marveled at my own skill.

As each mile passed, I continued to sing the funeral songs and deepen my visual of the event. I had now advanced the whole thing to a point where I would offer a video recording of myself, sharing my views on life and the gratitude I had for each experience. It was a bizarre twist to fantasize that I was speaking on gratitude while in such a deep, depressive state of self-pity. Somehow, this ongoing fantasy, so rich in detail and sensation, was making me feel alive in a very morbid and twisted way.

Next, I came upon Tony Podulsky's roadside mailbox. It was across the main highway and on the last portion of the route. Once again, the little voice began to speak to me. This time, it was direct: *"DECIDE! Do you want to live or do you want to die?"*

It was a matter-of-fact question that somehow shocked its way through this thick layer that had encrusted me. It penetrated deeply to the core of my heart to wake me from this spiraling experience, and I heard myself realize, "Wow...this is a really huge waste of time!"

My thoughts continued. Surely, I had things to do in my life and really needed to let go of this crazy indulgence and simply get on with living. What was wrong with me to fall so far into this bizarre indulgence? Somewhere deep within me, I also knew that a child would come.

Just like that, I decided to let it all go and start a fresh page. With this sudden renewed vigor and a sense of fresh air moving through my entire body, I felt what was beginning to resemble hope. It was as though I had become a witness in my own experience.

My body continued driving around the route, taking time to move all of the remaining mail from the back of my little S-10 pickup into the cab of the truck. I cleaned the whole truck up on the inside so efficiently with each stop, putting loose items in the glove box and placing the cassette with my funeral songs on the dash. This was peculiar behavior, acting as though I were battening down the hatches before a storm.

Then I hit the highway and began my stops on the right-hand side of the road, delivering bundles of mail into roadside boxes. As I got to this one mailbox, the little voice began to speak again. The next box I would be delivering to was on the left-hand side of the highway and the little voice simply said, *"You could wait."* I looked around at the traffic pattern. There was one lane on my side and two lanes approaching. There was a generous amount of room to move out onto the road and make the left turn into the next driveway. I pulled out.

Coming toward me was one of those old, antique cars, long and blue, a beautiful specimen of preserved history. It was slowing down, with the right-turn signal flashing. The driver was also turning into the driveway I was heading for. In the other lane, coming toward me was a semi truck and trailer, which was quite a ways back. Behind, in the distance, was a full-sized red Ford Bronco heading toward me in my lane. I was now aligned perfectly to make my turn into the driveway, and when the time was right, I would simply whip in as I had always done.

With one foot on the clutch and one on the gas, I was poised and ready to go, simply waiting for the blue antique car to complete its turn into the driveway. The little voice began again. *"You could always take the ditch."*

By this time, I felt annoyed. I was concentrating. What was with this little voice? It made me angry. The whole thing was perfectly managed and timed, and I would be long gone by the time this Bronco made it to me. But I noticed as I checked the rearview mirror that he was getting bigger and that he wasn't moving over to go around me.

I inched a little closer to the centerline and was now slowly rolling, ready to pop the clutch and be on my way. And then the whole thing changed. The old, antique car, instead of pulling into the driveway, pulled across the driveway and stopped. The driver had no idea what was going on around him as he blocked the whole entrance. There I was, in the middle of the highway, suddenly with no options.

Of course, this was all happening so fast, but somehow, the mind slowed it down to a point that every breath was captured deep in the memory banks. The Bronco was fully in the rearview mirror, hadn't moved an inch, and showed no signs of slowing. I had nowhere to go. The time was up. It was right there. The little voice in my head simply said, *"Relax and take the hit."*

In my mind, I imagined a bumper car cartoon experience, where I would get pushed forward and we would all walk away just fine. Instead, the Bronco hit the rear passenger side of my vehicle and literally drove underneath of it. As this happened, the front end of my vehicle launched upward and began its 360-degree full-circle spin backward in the air. At the same time, it rotated 180 degrees over toward the driver's side and onto its roof. I had my left hand firmly gripping the steering wheel, and like a cartoon character being colored, I felt a sensation of grey oozing from the center of my brain like paint pouring throughout my whole head. A feeling of coolness and full surrender engulfed me as the experience unfolded. That was the last thing I remembered.

My hand had been firmly gripping the steering wheel when my unbelted body flew backward, bending the steering wheel over to a forty-five-degree angle from the force. As I flew, I broke my seat and my head crashed through the extended cab's back window, denting the cab itself in the process.

Somehow, I managed to stay within the vehicle, and when it all settled to a stop, I was lying inside the truck, on the roof, which was now upside down on the road. As soon as I regained consciousness, all sorts of emotions swelled and I wanted to cry, but the little voice said, *"Now, crawl out."* Like an obedient child, I did.

In a pure state of shock, I weaved my way over to the antique vehicle, pointed out to the driver his error in blocking my way, and then proceeded to the Bronco. It was in the ditch on the left side of the road, upright and steaming. The driver was in shock, too, and had fared much worse than me. The emergency brake pedal had gone through his leg and he sat pinned amongst crumpled metal. His wife, who had been sleeping in the passenger seat, securely buckled in, was perfectly fine.

It seemed that they were managing a hotel at one of the small towns nearby, and they had been up all night. They were heading into the city for the day. Whether he fell asleep or was gazing into the field, I don't know, but he definitely made no attempt to brake or move around me in any way.

Luckily for all of us, my feet were on the clutch and the gas, and not the brake. It allowed both vehicles to free flow in the movement of the forces at play. My neck was pretty sore and stiff the next morning, and the muscles and ligaments of my left arm had been pulled quite significantly. Some inner ear damage affected my balance, but my injuries were so minor in the scope of possibility. It was an absolute miracle.

As I sat in the police car, giving my statement, I was in a blissful state of shock. I heard my voice recounting the details to this very kind and gentle officer, but the real me was sitting in pure amazement at the full realization of what I had just created.

All of my thoughts, all of my emotions, all of my fantasies, day after day after day, had led me to this perfect moment. A moment to meet with other individuals agreeing to play their part in a grand co-creation. What was even more deeply profound was that this little voice, the one that constantly spoke to me my entire life about things I thought so simple and meaningless, was profoundly and diligently trying to get me to let go of the whole experience before it came to be, giving me a choice of life or death and then aiding me as I insisted on having the full experience anyway.

We create our own reality. In every single moment, all of our thoughts and emotions, combined with intention and focus, carry us forward to experiences and manifestations that are being created by the very perfect union of these elements.

All things are energetic, including thoughts and emotions, and all energy moves in spiraling waveforms. As these waves interact with the sea of infinite energy potential of the void, the totality of energy that connects everything, this background of creative source births our next manifestations. Through the base elements of earth, water, fire, and air, perfect recipes are literally cooked up for us to experience. Co-creators seeking complimentary experience are drawn to us to share in the aspects we create. It is a wondrous and magical design.

While the knowledge of taking responsibility for what is in our lives can be difficult, it is also incredibly empowering, for the whole illustration shows us that we have a choice. I could have listened to that voice just once along the way and slowed down or stopped for a moment, and the entire scene would have changed. I was even asked to decide.

Most of the time, the signs are there for us to see the potentials of what we are creating. More often than not, the signs come in the attempt to steer us in certain directions, and we either discount them, ignore them, or fail to hear them altogether. The signs come in many forms that are always super obvious after the fact, when we have failed to listen. That would never be the case for me again. The little voice had my full and complete attention. I was in a state of awe and profoundly inspired by knowing that I could create anything I wanted.

# Chapter 2

My whole life had been a process of experiencing both ends of a spectrum, high highs and low lows. On the one hand, my mind was sharp and ambitious, always wanting to experience what I would imagine, but on the other hand, it was afraid. Life's specific circumstances always contributed to reinforcing the patterns I was cycling through, but on a fundamental level, I had simply been born swinging from one extreme to the other. It was what I had signed up for.

This tumultuous way of interfacing with life made me nervous and shy while dreaming of creating with all of the brilliance that was bubbling through. I longed to be special, but was deathly afraid of having too much attention placed upon me. And so began a pattern of seeking approval and worthiness from outside sources, and attention, but not too much.

I was a straight "A" student, perfect at regurgitating anything requested, but I didn't attempt to have any real opinions of my own. If they were wrong, that would risk my approval rating, and that was more important to me than anything. As a child, people were basically scary to me. There were conditions to be met to be liked, and if those weren't met, people could be downright mean to one another. I could not risk that.

As a child, my life at home was consistent. I was well cared for, fed, and clothed, but like most, our family had its share of dysfunction, too. We swept uncomfortable things under the rug and learned to suppress our emotions in order to keep things smooth and presentable on the surface. I was a master of holding my rattled self together and appearing perfectly okay on the outside.

But the truth was that as my body grew and I aged into adulthood, the frightened little girl inside remained. There was something wrong with me. I was defective. I believed that someday, someone was going to discover that I didn't grow up, and if someone were to find out before I could fix it, I would be in trouble. That trouble would include being shunned and ostracized. I couldn't bear that thought.

To cope, I got very good at being what I thought others wanted me to be. Filling a role at work was the perfect place for me to gain mass amounts of approval and have set roles I could simply act out. As long as I was the waitress in the restaurant, the mail girl in the country, or the controller and operations manager, I knew what to do, how to act, and what to say. Within those parameters was a freedom to express the brilliance that was bubbling through.

If someone asked me what I thought about anything else in the scope of human existence, I would panic like one on the hot seat of a major oral test. Instead of directly answering, I would maneuver a way to find out what that person thought and simply agree. Beyond being afraid to be wrong, I didn't even take the time to ask myself the questions.

Because my mind was so pliable, I could see everyone's points of view. I could follow opposing logics and see how easily people drew their conclusions. I had no vested interest in being right for what I thought, just included in what they thought. This made me the perfect mediator and bridge for people. I was neutral.

Emotions were the same. I could feel every one of them, and when someone would walk in a room, I could feel all of his or her emotions, too. I was highly empathic and had no idea what that was. I interpreted it as being completely unable to manage my own feelings. I would automatically contract my muscles tighter and deeper, and hold myself together a little longer. The feelings would pass, the resulting thought cycles of fear would slow, and a form a relaxation would come to my body. The breath would return to my lungs. I was always catching myself not breathing.

Running on pure adrenaline most of the time had me quite addicted to the sensation of it. Somehow, the reins I had placed on my external reactions were allowing me to find a sense of balance, but truthfully, it was more like containment. I contained, bottled, repressed, and compacted everything I felt into nice, neat, little compartments within my body and my brain, and then I laid a carpet over them and smiled.

And yet, there was the voice. It spoke to me off and on, always when I really needed it. It calmed me, it gave me perspective, and it guided me through years of being a completely different person on the inside than I was on the outside. It made me feel safe and special at the same time. And it was my secret sauce in everything I created in my work, for it would guide me effortlessly to the next sign and the next opportunity.

I was a person with her feet on both the gas and the brakes all the time. A tightly wound spring on high alert, beneath a facade of pleasant calm. To add to that, I drank excessive amounts of coffee to propel my energy through channels of work, amassing wealth and a position in the corporate world. My employees referred to me as "a little intense." That was an understatement.

One Friday morning, as I drove from our farm into the city for work, I became aware that my toes were gripping the insides of my shoes like claws. This was 7:00 a.m. and the day had just begun. And the little voice was back, preparing me. It was once again time to choose.

I was unhappy at the very core of my being. I had followed all of the rules and had attempted to play the game with finesse, all the while knowing that I simply didn't fit, all the while feeling defective in some way and certain that I was the only one suffering this affliction.

The next day, my son and I were weeding in the garden. The temperature was 30°C, which was great for killing weeds but terrible for a human standing on black soil. We quickly surrendered and headed for the coolness of the house, a couple of cold glasses of iced tea, and an afternoon movie.

My mood was quiet and reflective. I felt so emotionally drained and I had been trying to keep myself moving, as though that would somehow help me outrun the feeling that followed me like a cloud.

We plopped down in chairs in the living room and my mind sank in a deep, internal core, where a full-blown knowing filled every cell. I saw my life path as it was currently laid before me. The job, the plan of working hard and saving money, to then someday have fun, was heading in the direction of illness and unhappiness. I felt such defeat. I had tried really hard to live within the system my whole life—to hold myself together, to play by the rules of the game for acceptance and approval, and for the success that was promised. I had a lot of pleasure and enjoyment in watching my creations come to life, but I couldn't escape seeing that they simply weren't making me happy. The whole existence was geared to the benefit of a few, and while I swallowed the hook of success deep in my throat, I was now choking on its taste.

The man I loved was becoming the target of my urge to blame someone or something for my unhappiness, but in that moment, I knew it was all on me. Emotion swelled in my throat, the little voice returned. *"Turn on the TV."*

It was 3:00 p.m., and as PBS appeared on the screen, Wayne Dyer was walking back and forth across the stage, sharing about his latest book, *The Power of Intention.* He was carefully reminding me what I had learned so many years ago. I create my own reality. All of my thoughts, all of my emotions, and all of my intentions had brought me to this moment, and I could choose to change it.

Once again, hope breathed into every cell and invigorated me into a reading frenzy. *Your Erroneous Zones* was first, another book by Wayne Dyer. In this one, he trains you to observe your mind as it reacts, moving your awareness from being the mind to being the observer. Next was the *Control Freak,* a very clever book that challenges you to look for the control freaks in the crowd and then come to realize that it is really you it refers to. It was an obvious approach but somehow felt more polite than coming at you head on.

Self-awareness books turned to physics with *The Field*, *The Holographic Universe*, and more. These led to the *Biology of Belief*, and then it all exploded as I read multiple books per week, reinforcing ideas, remembering truths, and learning new methods to deal with what arose in my experience of life.

Not only did I apply these things to me, I applied them in business and watched the subtle energetics of my world become consciously aligned to my growing awareness of truth. Feng shui, visualization, meditation, and intention all became my tools.

My world was shifting in every way imaginable, and this was amazing because the world never made much sense to me. Although I managed financial responsibilities continuously, the economy seemed to be one snarled, confusing mess of terminology that somehow didn't add up. I thought it was me and my inability to comprehend complex concepts, but that was not the case.

One day, my husband walked out of his office, down a long hallway, and said, "Did you know that the world is basically run by a handful of people?"

Immediately, a question of his mental health whisked through my mind like a banner on the back of a plane.

Seeing the look in my eyes and knowing in every cell of his body how important it was that I grasp what he was saying, he wisely said, "Here, read this." And he handed me a small article.

Articles led to blogs and blogs led to books. I couldn't get enough of what he was giving me. A whole other version of the economic and historical reality began to appear like Avalon in the parting of the mists. The world began to make sense. Confusions about the economy and politics began to give way, dispelling my belief that there was something dysfunctional about my ability to understand and interface with the adult world. None of it had ever made sense to me or felt comfortable, and now I knew why—it was all lies.

In the end, political and economic agendas all boiled down to corporate interests. Notions of true health and happiness among the masses were intentionally unnerved and disrupted by fear campaigns of sensation, delivered through mainstream media.

Advertising told us that we weren't pretty enough, smart enough, successful enough, or happy enough unless we bought their products and services, and strived to all be the same. News told us to fear our neighbors and see the danger in everything.

The Western world had developed into a massive herd of sheep going to work each day so they could afford to consume and keep the whole machine going— a corporate machine that was literally owned by a handful of people.

My partner had a gift for seeing the world from the top down, a helicopter view of the situation, seeing patterns and connections between things—and all of the crap that attempted to hide them. He was born seeking truth and justice, and was driven to swim against the stream.

Dealing with my partner could be like rubbing up against sandpaper. It would be abrasive and uncomfortable, but you always came out cleaner and smoother for the experience. He has been one of my greatest teachers.

We met when I was eighteen. I waitressed at a local coffee shop on the main floor of an office building, and one day, as I was setting the restaurant for lunch, I felt him coming. My usual routine was to come in early, crank the volume on the stereo, and get into my flow of dancing the place into form. To me, waitressing was a big game of conducting all of the elements involved so that everything would be perfectly timed and beautifully harmonious. I loved playing this role. It was fun and it was fantastic money, and I was good at it.

That day, I found my senses unusually heightened, as though I was trying to stretch my awareness all the way out of the glass windows that wrapped around the restaurant. Then I heard it. It was the deep, throaty sound of truck exhaust, not too loud that it was obnoxious, but just loud enough that you felt the vibration in your body, and it was exciting. My ears were piqued and tuned to follow the sound as I continued setting up cups and saucers.

The next time I looked out of the south window, I saw the vehicle parked right in front of my gaze. And leaning into the passenger door was a man, reaching for items across the seat. All I saw was the back of his body and his perfectly fitting jeans. Every cell in my body woke up in a way that I had never experienced before.

Lunch began and the customers reined all of my attention to the tasks. The next time I looked out of the window, the truck was gone. I didn't know why, but I could not get this man out of my head. I hadn't even seen his face, and yet, every cell and every sense stretched to seek his contact. Days passed and no sign of him or his vehicle. Until one day, mid-afternoon, he walked in the front doors of the restaurant, and my body confirmed that it was him.

We stood in the entrance face-to-face. The charge was electric and mutual, and the little voice in my head matter-of-factly declared, *"This will be hard, but it will be worth it."* It was right on both accounts.

We came together on some deep connection through many lifetimes. It was powerful on every level, and absolutely predestined, but we had come together in this life to perfectly play out dysfunction. We did an exceptional job at that. We were great at manifesting and focusing our energies into joint business opportunities, and in our union, we amassed a great deal of resources. I became stepmom to a wonderful young girl only eight years my junior, and then eight years after that, our son was born.

Areas of our partnership were easy, but most were challenging. It was hard, but it was worth it on every level you could imagine.

This man challenged me to think for myself, to stand up for myself, and to be confident in myself. He opened my eyes to the real, three-dimensional world as I was already opening them to the energetic and intuitive world. Because of my journey with him, I am both grounded in manifestation and connected to the full realms of source. Plus, I have beautiful children. I will forever be grateful, and while I would do things much differently if the clock were turned back, I would most definitely have still went down that road.

# Chapter 3

I remember the day when I was walking on my treadmill in the shop on the farm. My partner came in, leaned against the wooden potato bin, and took a nice, long breath to center himself. Whenever he began to speak to me from this point, fully relaxed, centered and aligned, I knew that what he would say would come from the depths of his truth, and that it was important to him that I listen. It was easy to pay full attention to his words.

I was already deep into a flow of transformation. All of the books I had read and all of the practices I had implemented in observing myself were already bringing me to becoming more comfortable within my own skin, more accepting of my nature, and less like an outcast. In addition to that, the knowledge of how the world really worked was prompting me to realize that I was walking within two worlds at once. Straddling the abyss that separated them was a challenge.

Once my partner knew that he had my full attention, he simply said, "It's now or never. Either we sell the farm now for whatever price we can get or we stay and make a life here with all of the development happening around us. But what you need to know is that the whole system is going to crash and we are almost at the peak." This was April 2007.

This man saw the impending economic crash years ahead of its arrival. By looking at the bigger patterns and the simple truths within them, it became easy for him to predict results and consequences as they were unfolding. This was his natural gift and we ensured that our life supported him with time for his further self-education in this area. He kept his finger on the pulse of the sources he had scouted and had built a well-established protocol for managing how the world would affect us.

We had already come to the conclusion that we would sell the farm a couple of years prior. We set a price for the land, and while the price seemed logical in the current market, it simply wasn't selling. What I was hearing was, if we didn't sell now, we wouldn't sell for any price, and that was simply not an option for me. I was ready for change.

The land we had purchased was beautifully located on the southwest slope of Richmond Hill, west of Grande Prairie. We had a lovely view of the mountains to the west. Although they were eighty miles off in the distance, you could see the range against the horizon. When the air was just a certain magical way, it would create a mirage and the mountains would feel like they were at the foot of our property. It was beautiful!

We had purchased this land many years prior and built a beautiful existence in the country. We had a big garden, a shop, every tool you could imagine, and machinery that was magically resurrected over and over and over again. Our tranquil pond was spring fed and stocked with rainbow trout. Our place was home to all kinds of wildlife—moose, deer, rabbits, coyotes, squirrels, geese, and even bears and blue heron on occasion. All in all, our life on this quarter section was the perfect blend of lifestyle and location.

Several years after we bought the property, the county decided to zone some of the surrounding land as industrial. A major road led from the highway directly to an existing industrial community, and it made sense to them to continue to develop the entire strip all the way back to the highway. Our property bordered this road.

This created two effects. First, it made it so that we got to listen to the clanking of drill stem pipe in the yards surrounding us, and second, it inflated the value of our property. It's important to know that I had envisioned us sitting on the porch of our house, rocking and gazing at those mountains well into our aging years. Every tree we planted and every stone we collected marked a deep love for the land itself. Our lives were still way too busy to fully enjoy the property and the lifestyle, but we were very much in a nurturing and supportive element.

Each year, I would work the soil of my lush and fertile garden. Then I would load my garden seeder with fresh seeds and begin walking up and down the rows. This was the most perfect invention. Two wheels, a long handle and a seed reservoir with an attachment for different size seeds. A metal rod could be set out to the side to drag along the ground, marking a perfect line for the next row as you walked and seeded the current one.

This contraption saved an enormous amount of time as it dug the furrow for the seed, and then covered after carefully dropping seed after seed in perfect spacing. The problem was that when you had a two-acre garden and too much ambition, you would end up with four or five 150' rows of carrots, or so I was told.

I loved that garden and looked so forward each January to mapping out the rotational plan, ordering from the seed catalogue and waiting for spring to arrive.

My world was shifting in every way imaginable. Coupled with my growing education in the truth of the 3-D economic world, this left me feeling like Neo walking around in the matrix after ingesting the red pill. It was impossible to live in both realities, and yet, by the time my partner walked into the shop that day, and spoke to me as I continued walking on that treadmill, I had already fully committed in my heart to unplugging from the matrix, entirely.

His words resonated as truth in every cell of my body. My inner voice said, *"Sell."* As soon as the decision was made, I began the process of packing and organizing all of our items. Once the voice speaks to me, everything happens, and I saw no need to wait.

Even though we still had no buyer, I knew that we were already gone, and this was my chance to sort out our whole life and prepare for next steps that would come. On some level, I also knew that he and I would be parting ways, and that this was a graceful and necessary step to prepare for that inevitability. I suppose I didn't allow myself to consciously know that, and the truth was that I loved that man, still do, always would, but the dysfunction between us had grown to a point where it simply needed to stop, and the only way to stop it was to actually stop it. This was where my mind was really at, and so I went forward, stepping directly into it.

I catalogued all of the possessions we had in the house and left the farmyard decisions to my partner. In less than one month, we had found the buyer and signed the papers. Now we had four months to move.

A sense of freedom and excitement that only came from the chance to start a whole new life had permeated me. I was completely blissed-out! I gave notice at my job and began a long process of preparing a smooth transition for the next person to step in. I took great care in leaving tools for the transition, for I loved the business and all of the people I worked with. I knew that I would miss the freedom of creative expression the owners so freely gave me in managing, but I felt a hundred percent complete with the experience and was ready to go.

The sale of the land was affording me a chance to simply relax and take time off—time to decompress from years and years of nonstop work, time to really find out who I was and what would fill my heart. Everything was changing rapidly and I was invigorated to the depths of my soul.

Whenever the little voice was being directly followed, things would unfold like magic, like the land buyer being found through a synchronistic conversation at a business course I attended. The decisions and choices I was making at this time in my life seemed to be the result of some tractor beam attraction drawing me in, rather than my mind having any strategic involvement at all. Things appeared effortlessly, inviting me to relax and just say yes to the guidance. That was when Sedona called me.

# Chapter 4

I had never been on my own vacation before, but somehow, I was being called to treat myself to a week of pampering and luxury, and this week would be without my family. My partner was happy to think of me on an adventure of my own, and that support was the permission I needed. This was a time of great happiness for all of us as we prepared for the changes and stared absolute freedom in the face.

I typed the words "pampering spa vacation" into the Google screen, and the Miiamo Spa in Sedona, Arizona, popped up. It looked absolutely decadent. I recalled that I had been through Sedona as a child, on an excursion to collect my snowbird grandmother from her winter adventures in the Phoenix area. I remembered that it was beautiful, with red mountains, and that my sister, Valerie, who was with us on the journey, was so deeply moved by its energies.

Sedona then became the focus, and soon, everything Sedona was all around me. Magazine articles, newspaper images, adventure brochures. Out of nowhere, the name of Sedona was popping up everywhere. My search for the perfect getaway continued. After much Web investigation, I began chatting with a company named Sedona Soul Adventures.

Run by Tom and Debra Margrave, they specialized in assisting people to experience direct contact with their souls. What had begun as a spa resort concept had now grown into a spiritual adventure. I was really excited.

After talking with Mary, an angel guide, I signed up for a week of sessions. Mary, a highly intuitive channel and heart-centered woman, connected with my higher aspects to see what would benefit me and then put the retreat together in the perfect order of events. Off I went, mid-July, and once again, I was in the company of my sister, Valerie.

Valerie enjoyed the beauty of the land and galleries, painting landscapes and soaking up the energy, while I spent the day moving from session to session, in a seemingly perfect deepening of experiences.

It began with a soul reading from Joan Kidd. Joan was born aware and fully connected to source. She has the ability to communicate directly with your soul, providing divine information. After getting comfortable in her space and setting the intention for a safe and beautiful session, she asked me the question, "How is your marriage?"

I answered, "Well, it has its ups and downs, but overall, it's good."

Then she said, "Well, the first thing we have to do is get you to stop lying to yourself."

Joan was straightforward. She was kind and loving, but her duty was to your soul and so she conveyed the messages exactly as she received them.

It became abundantly clear in those first few moments that no one was going to flatter me with stories of being the reincarnation of Cleopatra or some other ego-boosting notion. We were going to get down to a truth and a depth that I, in my own conscious psyche, had masked in myself. I felt both fear and relief in the same moment. My life was going to change and this was what I yearned for.

Joan spent the next hour or so connecting with my soul and telling me of the truths that the essence of myself wanted my mind to know. Much of them were deeply inspiring and uplifting messages of the beauty and potential of what I could do and create. These were grand visions that resonated but also intimidated me.

I left after many tears of release, feeling empty of resistance, and surrendered to truth in a way not ever experienced. Joan saw me for who I was and reflected back a picture of both love and truth. It contained all of the beauty and all of the illusions. I had work to do. I felt seen in a way that I had not yet known. I felt accepted without judgment. And I felt excited of where my life would lead.

Joan's reading was followed by a *lomi-lomi* oil massage, and the moment I lay face down on the woman's table, I began deep sobbing and released throughout the entire nurturing session. I couldn't have stopped if I had tried.

After a few hours of cold compresses on puffy eyes, I managed to spend the evening at dinner with Valerie, sharing my experiences and looking to the next morning. I felt a relaxation at the deepest level and the presence of mind that only comes from being conscious in the moment.

The next day began with an astrology reading, and into the room entered Evan, this large man with a hint of a New York accent. Jewish and outspoken, he exuded an excitement in meeting me, and being able to share and observe how the planets were affecting my evolution and unfoldment. He was opinionated and certain of everything he spoke. I liked him instantly.

He provided a new doorway for me to peer into my tendencies and see my potential. It was profoundly encouraging and the perfect way to begin to see the next phase of my life unfold. Dreams of writing and sharing knowledge were supported by the placement of planets in my chart, including a *Yod*, or Finger of God, which lined everything up and pointed me toward the path of sharing spiritual knowledge. While the how and when were unclear to me, the message was very exciting.

In the afternoon, I knocked on the door of Wanda's house, and as it flung open, I saw a tall, beautiful blonde woman, gracefully dressed in a long gown. A childlike, mischievous smile spread across her face as she welcomed me in. Wanda was the perfect depiction of a playful and friendly mystic, an interpretation quite close to the mark.

"You are supposed to be here for an emotional clearing," she said and then paused. "I don't think that's why you're here. Why don't you come with me?"

I followed her in through the house to her session room. It was a beautiful room, decorated in light-pink hues with lace draping accenting angelic figurines and images. It was soft, gentle, and cozy.

On each side of a massage table were chairs and we settled into them to begin chatting. We caught up to what I had already experienced in my short time in Sedona, and then I was invited up onto the table. I stretched out and relaxed as Wanda began to tune into what would be first.

Wanda could see. She could see beyond the veils of normal vision and into the multidimensional layers of light and form. She could see right inside the body and then feel into what was stored and held in the very tissues of it. We began with my connection to my son.

I had been wrestling with my choices as a mother. I wanted to be the best mother that I could, but I was struggling with all of the changes we were now putting our son through. We pulled him from school and enrolled him in a virtual online program that he could do while we roamed around, exploring our new life. Was this the best thing for him? Was I making mistakes? Would he be okay, away from all of his friends? It was heavy in my emotions and weighed on my heart.

Wanda shared that a long cord connected him and me, like an energetic umbilical, and that at any time I ever wanted, I could close my eyes and connect directly with his soul. She led me into this experience. It was amazing. As soon as we started, I felt his presence all around. He and I were very connected, easily reading each other's thoughts and emotions regardless of distance. Wanda tracked alongside me as I journeyed down this new road.

I began to hear his soul talking to me. He was okay and he wanted me to know that. His life was unfolding exactly as he planned, and I needed to worry less about him and focus my energy on my own unfolding development. He was already directing his own experience and I was good to trust all that was happening. We were co-creating the experience anyway. He was as grateful to be my son as I was to be his mom. I cried with such gratitude.

In addition, a tremendous relief filled me as I watched my own perception of this young man switch from the little boy I had tried to preserve him as, to the wise and divine soul that, in most ways, was my teacher rather than the other way around. If this were the only thing I had experienced in Sedona, it would have been enough. But there was more.

We moved away from this experience to where Wanda now was directing my breath. She asked me to draw the breath up through the soles of my feet as I inhaled, bringing it all the way to my heart. On every inhale, I felt the sensation and followed it with my awareness from the bottoms of my feet, up the legs and torso, right into the heart center. On every exhale, I seemed to expand.

After a few breaths, she asked that I also bring breath in through the top of my head, the crown, and mix it with the upward breath in my heart center. Again, I followed the sensation of the flow of breath from the crown down and into the heart. I was able to follow both flows as they now entered my body and met in the heart center.

Cells in my body began to tingle, starting lightly, but then escalating out of my control. Charley horse cramping in my calves began as my hands crumpled up with deformity. My wrists bent forward and the fingers took on odd projections. My ankles bent inward and my toes began to curl. I was panicking on the inside and I spoke out for help.

This was tetany, a term used to describe the physical experience of hyper excitation of nerves and muscles. Energetically, this was the flow of energy finding blockages and moving them to exit out of the extremities.

Wanda stopped me and had me stand to the side of the massage table, breathing long and deep as I worked out the charley horses in my legs. Everything calmed down and my limbs returned to normal. She handed me a glass of water and a Trace Minerals Vitamin C packet. I mixed them together and drank the whole glass. She explained that minerals and electrolytes would assist me in running the energy. Then I returned to the table and resumed the breath.

Again, the flow of sensation was coming in through the bottoms of my feet and the top of my head, moving into my heart on every inhale. Wanda then instructed me to exhale through my arms and out of my hands. The sensations returned, vibrating and circulating energy currents throughout my body. Only this time, no lock-ups were occurring. The energy was free flowing and building, and it was both relaxing and mesmerizing me at the same time. I had no idea what was really happening to me, but it was very special and I felt invigorated and excited.

Then it kicked up to an entirely new level. As though someone had flipped the "open" switch in my body, a stove-pipe-sized channel of energy opened from the bottoms of each foot to the base of my spine, and from the base of my spine and out of the top of my head. Energy poured in through the feet and shot out of the crown. It poured in through the crown and shot out of the soles of the feet, all at the same time.

As it passed each other, swirls formed and it flooded down my arms and exploded out of my palms. The frequency and pattern of intensity moved like it had a spirit of its own. It no longer flowed with the breath; it just coursed through my body in a current of its own making. I was not sure I was even breathing, as I lay, mouth wide open, in a pure and absolute state of awe.

Someone or something had hooked me up to the universe, and the universe was flooding through my entire body. I had opened a portal, Wanda explained. My brain was sparkling and I was sure that light was pouring from every cell. The streams of energy that left my palms were divine and I was confident that anyone in the presence of my hands would be healed instantly. Life was never going to be the same.

Wanda held up Barbara Brennan's book, *Hands of Light*, and showed me the cover. Upon it was a set of hands with light shining out in beams. She said, "This is what your whole body looks like."

I knew that it was true. I felt set aglow. I felt cleaned. I felt radiant. I felt like the goddess herself.

More followed in Wanda's session, which could be the topic of another whole book, but the energetic awakening I received on that table was what opened me to a higher state of being. I was elevated and activated to a new level of awareness and consciousness. All of those years when my little voice would come in and out, I perceived it as divine guidance from an outside source. Now I knew, it was me, the real me, the true and divine essence of my soul, trying to get inside my body and move me into its point of awareness rather than my mind's. Now as the whole body was opened to the flow of the divine, I was fully present in every cell of my body. It was wild!

The little voice had led me to let go of my existing life, job, home, and possessions to come to Sedona to be jolted awake—an experience of such profound mind shift that it would launch me in an entirely new direction.

Cleared on mental, emotional, and physical levels, a channel within me was now activated. I would never confuse myself and think I was my body or my mind. My eyes had been opened in ways that I couldn't have imagined. I was in my element, immersed in the explorations of Sedona's esoteric offerings. I had found my home and I knew would be back. The little voice told me. Next time, I would bring my family.

# Chapter 5

The day following my visit to Wanda's, I went to experience my first formal breath work session. It was based on the teachings of Stansilov Grof and was called Holotropic Breathwork.

In this practice, one begins with a deep discussion of the practice and its effects. Then a pattern of circular breathing begins that alters one's state of awareness. Vast amounts of oxygen and *prana*, the rejuvenative life force, entering my body began to bring on the sensations of energy flowing through all of my channels, vibrating all of my cells. This was not as dramatic as the day at Wanda's, but the same idea and flow patterns.

The holotrophic breath work session went on for a couple of hours in the loving care of a beautiful feminine soul. She held a nurturing and supportive space in which I felt completely safe. I reached states of profound awareness, felt the presence of angelic beings and the movement of stuck energy out of every pathway. These were all experiences that were completely new to this mind.

I remember having to stop a few times to go to the washroom and marveled at the volume of water that could pass through my body as I literally cleared tissues, cells, and energetic forms in this stream of release. My body, mind, and spirit were being purified and the instrument was the breath. I was so blown away by this point that nothing more was required on my trip. Yet, there was still more to come.

Next, I was sent to the Oak Creek Canyon to a beautiful oasis known as Your Heart's Home. Resident goddess, owner, and steward of this precious property, Ranjita Ryan, met me and led me to chat in her quaint and magically decorated A-frame home. The house was perched on the side of a mountain, with Oak Creek below. The sounds of the water and the smells of nature filled and nurtured all of my senses. We talked of my life and all that I had experienced on this trip so far. We began our session by pulling cards from various fairy and goddess decks.

The cards gave a flavor of what energies were in play in my current life, what transitions were coming, and how they might play out. They also revealed what my soul was yearning for. The general theme was that a dramatic change of a difficult nature was coming and that the wild woman, the BABA YAGA energy, wanted to be revealed. Baba Yaga represented the unbridled, passion-filled being that lay suppressed within me.

I was timid and shy unless playing a role, while underneath I was filled with passion and certainty of who I truly was. Somehow, I was split in my nature, as I had steadily suppressed and repressed all pleasurable and happy occurrences. I was more afraid to be happy and experience a life filled with pleasure than I was to suffer the pain and contraction I was now enduring.

I had become completely comfortable in the role of a martyr and I had attracted a lot of people into my life to assist me with this dynamic. The deeper part of me was ready to hear this and that was why Sedona called me in. Today was going to be more difficult, this I could see.

We stepped into Ranjita's greenhouse, filled with sacred objects, statues, crystals, and shamanic tools. Flowers bloomed in the glass atrium. Once again, I was led onto a massage table and then guided deep within my own imaginings as we journeyed to visualize my heart's home.

What did it look like? It was a cave. At the bottom of the cave was a pool of white milk. I knew it had to be significant and not "made up," for I would never have consciously chosen a pool of milk. It seemed strange at first.

Within my heart's home, Ranjita led me to see three aspects of myself: the divine feminine, the divine masculine, and the divine child.

The masculine was strong, tall, and handsome, and yet a bit wounded on one side of his body. He had a slight limp, but nothing that really slowed him down. He looked a bit tired but still running on a level of reliability that removed doubt from any perception of his capabilities. The little child was shy, quiet, and a bit sad, but the divine feminine was in bad shape.

She appeared dirty and skinny in a ragged dress, dark circles under her eyes, and she looked as though she had been living in this dark cave for an eternity. She was neglected and in a state of self-imposed poverty—poverty of the soul more so than even the physical realm. She was tattered and torn, and I realized in those moments that I had been severely mistreating her as I chose to participate and endure in the life I had created with my partner.

For many years, I had projected my unhappiness out onto my partner. I behaved like one certain that if only he would change his ways, I would be happy. I knew in my soul that I was responsible for my own reality, and now I was staring that reality in the face. My inner divine trinity was playing out the whole story right before my eyes in this cave of my heart. I imagined sitting on the floor of the cave, hands cradling my face as my feet dipped and swung in the pool of milk. It was a sorry state of being for my eyes to see.

Ranjita guided me as I talked with the aspects and initiated a conversation between the masculine and feminine parts. They battled out their complaints to one another of how each felt unfairly treated, and then moved into expressing their true needs. My masculine aspect had been such a profound player in my life, always pushing forward and taking all of the necessary actions required to manage and control the aspects around me. Intent on serving as the protector and doer, this aspect was a warrior of immense intelligence and capability. The feminine, for the most part, was ignored and underutilized.

Her natural intuition was stifled for logic and external approval, running off programming that feminine was weak and secondary in the world. I gazed at the scene and felt shame for such mistreatment. My whole life would change now. It already was.

I had already said good-bye to a six-figure income, my land, and soon, my community. My eyes were opened to the subtle world in a way that I could never revert back from. My real path lay before me and the little voice I had heard my whole life was now known to me as me. I was ready to return to Canada. I had work to do.

# Chapter 6

Upon my return, we immersed deep in preparing for our auction. It seemed the most logical method to get rid of our farming possessions rather than to attempt to store them for some later date and unknown project. Plus, it would further liquidate things to place our resources in the gold bullion investment we had targeted as our safe haven. My partner was brilliant in these matters and my little voice was in full support.

The auction was my first. What fun it was to touch everything and clean it up, and then present it to the world. By the time the day arrived, we had amassed a literal country store of good-quality used items, and had enjoyed a pleasant journey down memory lane. In fact, many of the people who wandered onto the property that day remarked that they had never seen such an overall good quality of items. We did well. Some things, like our $400 barbecue, sold for $50, but a deck truck we owned sold for $10,000 over what we expected, and that made up for all of the little items going cheaply. All in all, we were happy and we were free.

Off we went, the three of us, in our new pickup, pulling a small utility trailer filled with items that we could not live without. We were ready for a whole new world of adventure… Sedona bound we went.

My son and partner both did soul adventures, and it would be foolish of me to attempt to explain their experiences. But it was fun to see the magic as it shone through their eyes. It was a good time for us all.

I revisited Wanda in hopes of another profound and ecstatic experience of energy pouring through my body. Instead, she led me to experience memories I had buried early in my life, some time around the age of five. An experience had occurred that my little mind could not comprehend or bear, and so the wisdom of the autopilot system of my mind simply put it all in a tight, little container within the brain itself and I moved on. I was completely unaware that the occurrence had ever happened; yet this experience was the undercurrent that shaped my life.

The story itself is irrelevant and I have purposefully left it out because we all have stories to identify with that can be inserted here. It is never about the details. The resulting brain patterns and subconscious programs are what are important.

A little mind of a child is a delicate instrument, operating at slowed brain wave states that don't afford discernment or question. They simply record, like an auto playback machine. Everything simply gets written in. When an experience threatens the mental health, the autopilot mind, in its brilliant design, simply dissociates from the experience so the delicate psyche can continue to live.

What I uncovered, as Wanda led me by the energetic hand to the memory, put me in a state of disbelief. There, in the tissues of my actual physical body, lay an experience carefully compacted and hidden from my awareness. How could anyone suppress a memory so painful? I couldn't imagine it possible.

But it was like a puzzle piece suddenly dropped into the center of a picture, finally revealing the whole image, an image that made perfect sense. As I stared at it, felt it, and witnessed the images flashing through my mind, there was a deep knowing that this was truth. My little voice was right there and whole awarenesses were bursting simultaneously like fireworks in the center of my brain. If someone had told me this, I would never have believed him or her. This was the only way I could remember.

The puzzle piece explained so many things. I now knew why my whole life had unfolded in the way it had. The only thing I wanted was to extract every trace of its effects from every aspect of me—my body, my mind, and my soul. I felt toxic and even more uncomfortable in my own skin than I had ever been.

Off to the bookstore I went in search of the next great teaching to help me extract every aspect of pain I was now feeling. Deepak Chopra's book, *Perfect Health*, introduced me to Ayurvedic practices, and this led me to *Pancha* Karma, a method of cleansing practiced a few times a year. A Google search further led me to local Sedona practitioner, Avani Sukhadia.

Avani lovingly took me on a journey of diet and herbs, and decadent massage treatments. From dry brushing with oil massage, to *shirodhara*, where warm oil is dripped over the eyebrow center in a steady, soothing stream, to herb-infused steams to nourish and pamper all of the senses, I was treated like royalty. A special diet was prescribed along with practices that enhanced the overall cleanse process.

When we completed, she said, as though dishing out a prescription, "You need Yoga. Go to 7 Centers Yoga Arts."

I had never been to a Yoga class in my life, but I obediently listened, still firm on my quest to rid myself of any and all effects of the buried information.

At the same time, my mind began to question the validity of the information I had uncovered. What if it weren't true? What kind of person imagines this kind of thing? What could possibly be wrong with me? I began to go to different intuitives to see if they could verify its truth. It was coming out in all of the readings.

Then my mind began to reason that they were only picking it up because I was imagining the possibility. My mind was seeking every potential reason to discount and rebury the information.

Off I went to Yoga. Seven Centers is a Yoga arts school that predominantly trains and certifies teachers, but they also offer a regular class schedule for the community and visitors. I began going to the 8 a.m. class held in their yurt. A new teachers' training group was immersed in a thirty-day intensive in the main building.

I went every day and this beautiful, young, and wise *yogini* named Mira Murphy was my teacher. Mira's heart radiates with such light and beauty that anyone around her feels the gift of this attunement. In my good fortune, many mornings, I would be the only student to show up, and so Mira gave me private instruction with a focus on breathing deep into the back.

Back breathing was part of Rama Joyti Vernon's Yoga. Rama is the person responsible for bringing *Iyengar* to North America and for starting *Yoga Journal* on her kitchen table. The back breathing concept allows one to send *prana*, the rejuvenative and healing life force that travels with the breath, into the depths of the back body to illuminate the subconscious storehouse of impressions and programs. By focusing the breath into these areas, you literally feel physical openings and expansions of space form in the body. All impressions that have been blocked up or stored are invited to be released. Sometimes, the release comes with sensation and simple witnessing, and sometimes it is emotional and even filled with memory. This was going to really help me.

Day after day, I would come and Mira would instruct me through a series of postures to open my whole body while sending the breath around. I felt amazing. My body was beginning to feel like one whole unit again, instead of a collection of body parts tied together through joints. There was flow, mobility, and a relaxed energy. I knew I had found something that would become part of my life's practice. I would be going to lots of Yoga classes.

The *asana* instruction was coupled with wise awarenesses that Mira would suggest for contemplation. This young twenty-two-year-old was rapidly becoming the wisest person I knew. One day, I stopped in the middle of the practice and asked, "How did someone so young get to be so wise?"

Her reply: "My mom is kinda into Yoga."

It turned out that Mira's mom was Rama, and that from the time of conception, Mira was deeply immersed in Yoga's benefits.

Mira observed my natural integration of the work and quickly encouraged me to take the teachers' training. I had no interest in becoming a Yoga teacher, so I could not see the point, but Mira explained that many people take it for the retreat experience. "The thirty days of retreat and time away from' one's life, while diving deeply into a healing practice, is life changing," she said.

Somewhere deep inside of me, I heard, "Time away from one's own life," and "life changing," and knew I would do it. This was October. I plunged ahead, planning for an April training the following year. Thirty days to immerse in practices that would cleanse the very tissues of my body. This was exactly what would fix me! I was sure.

Meanwhile, I was also exploring other avenues to heal. Wanda had initiated a level one training for medical intuitive mastery. I had no interest in being a medical intuitive, nor did I believe I had the skill, but I would participate in anything Wanda was doing. She was amazing!

Several significant things happened during the three-day training, but two specifically stood out. Each had profound messages within them that made no sense at the time, but would reveal an actual map of the charted course I was following. The first occurred as the training began.

Wanda started by assisting us to clear and open the third eye region. She would look into our body and see what was blocking it on an energetic level, and then assist us in clearing it. When she got to mine, she saw an etheric metal plate covering my third eye center. She energetically removed it and placed it in the palm of my hand.

I closed my eyes and was surprised to see it pop into my field of awareness. Everything in Wanda's presence was easy. She told me to look it over carefully, draw a picture of it, and write down anything that came to me as I did.

It was quick. On the face of the plate was a triangle with the tip pointed downward. Inside was a circle and another encompassed it on the outside. The words, *"Sun alignment"* and *"Shift is coming"* echoed in my head. I wrote them down but had no idea what they or the symbol meant. Wanda turned back to me and together, her and my little voice said, *"This is about Peru. Write that down."*

The other thing that happened occurred on the second day. Earlier in the day, we were imagining our right hands as crystals. We were instructed to imagine whatever crystal popped into our minds as soon as we closed our eyes. Mine was a beautiful, clear quartz. Upon the fingers and the center of the palm, we were instructed to imagine sets of eyes. Mine were big, doughy eyes, each a unique brilliant color, with long, curled eyelashes. You know, the kind that ironically only little boys seem to get. My right hand was beautiful and the picture in my mind was vivid.

Wanda instructed us to place our hand upon our thigh and imagine it sinking deep into our leg. With eyes closed, we were to imagine what we would see. It was easy. I sunk my awareness in and saw smooth and silky muscles, and beneath that, I saw joints and bones. We would isolate a specific point and then attempt to sink our awareness even deeper within the area.

I found the whole thing so fun because it came to me quickly and I never thought I would be able to do something I deemed so special. I really believed that one needed to be gifted to use intuitive practices, but

Wanda was showing me that we all have the capability to open these skills, naturally, within us. I was ready and she was the perfect teacher.

Wherever a density or sore spot was found, we would dive deeper into it and then begin to feel it with our feelings. Emotions, thoughts, ideas, and pictures would reveal themselves, sharing the story of the origin of the current tissue condition. In Wanda's work, she guides people into these awarenesses so they can remove the unwanted emotions, stories, thoughts, and beliefs and replace them with love and healing colors. I was excited. I was good at this and it was easy. Maybe I was gifted, my mind thought. We took a break for lunch.

Lunch concluded and we were back at it. This time, we would work with the left hand. Curious about what beauty my left hand would possess, I found myself shocked when it turned out to be a black, shiny crystal. Not only was it black, but it protruded beyond the boundaries of my hand. When I placed it on my leg in preparation to sink it in, it simply dove and began cruising around my body on its own will. I was startled and scared.

Where the eyes were to be found instead revealed the slits of snake eyes. The whole thing was creepy and I didn't know what to think. Wanda watched us all as we journeyed with the left hand, and when we concluded and I opened my eyes, she looked at me, held up her hand to signal me to be patient, and said, "I know. We'll deal with that in a minute."

She circulated the room, asking each person to share his or her story, and saved mine for last. My mind was still reeling with worry about what I had done wrong to cause this to surface.

Soon, her attention was on me and I described the experience to the whole group. Wanda said, "It's time for you to go into the void. This is about the void."

She had me close my eyes and take some relaxing breaths and then imagine complete blackness. I was in space and heading toward a black hole. Like one would imagine a wormhole or tube, I found myself inside the blackness, moving forward into an unknown. I was nervous.

Wanda assured me that she was right with me and could see everything I was experiencing, and that gave me courage. I continued forward in my mind. But the nervousness was growing into fear as we continued. I could feel Wanda's energetic hand in mine, so I knew she was right there, but something strange was happening to my mind.

It felt as though my personality, my actual identity was disintegrating and turning to dust, the dust blowing off into the wind. I was disappearing. I was disappearing! My mind began to freak out and race. Wanda reassured me and I kept moving forward.

Now, we were at a portal, a doorway, the center of the black hole and an entrance to the other side of it. Wanda asked me to step through and share what I experienced. I moved my awareness through the entrance. My awareness was all that was left. My body and my mind had evaporated in the channel leading to this core, and now the essence of me simply expanded.

It expanded into the sea of sparkly, blue-white light that lay beyond the portal I crossed through. As though I were a drop of sparkly dye merging into the sea, I simply spread and became the sea itself. A feeling of bliss and absolute connection with the entire universe filled me with such joy and love in a way I had never experienced before. I was free! I was free of my mind, my worries, my ideas, my fears, my hopes—everything. I had no form. I had no boundaries. I was pure god-source essence itself, fully merged into oneness with everything. I was home.

Then I heard Wanda's voice. "Now take that sea of sparkly, blue-white light by the corner, as if it were a big blanket, and begin to drag it behind you as we journey back through the black hole."

I didn't want to go, but I was already following her voice.

A few moments later, I was back in the room on my chair as Wanda instructed me to imagine this blanket of light wrapped all around me.

"You're in shock. Just sit and breathe, and when you feel ready, write down everything you just experienced. Someday, you will take people on that journey. Take notes. You are a black-hole walker," she said.

Whatever that meant.

Wanda was always telling me things about what would come for me. I was fascinated and bewildered at the same moment. But mostly, I liked that she saw something in me that I could not. I liked seeing myself in the reflection of her words. I liked the deepening experience of connecting with the essence that I was. It felt so blissful to be fully expanded. What was this? I wanted more.

# Chapter 7

The following spring, my partner, my son, and I ventured over to Egypt. We traveled with a group from Sedona, touring all major sites and cruising up the Nile to visit temples along its banks.

Books like *Fingerprints of the Gods*, by Graham Hancock, and all of the works of Drunvallo Melchizedek prepared me for the sights I was to see and dispelled any illusion that the pyramids were built by humans.

As we stood at their base, the sheer size of the blocks and perfection of the structure removed any shadow of nonsense that we humans could have accomplished such a feat. And if the logic of that was not enough, the energy emitting from the stones themselves was enough to defy the standard story as it activated knowledge and memory deep within our cells. I was blown away.

Each site felt different and invoked a unique response. Ever since the day on Wanda's table, when my channel was opened, I could sense my world through the vibrating fields of energy interacting with my body. Everything is made of energy and each has a unique signature that results in its form. I could feel this as I interacted with my world now. The sacred sites of the world are like Disneyland to one who feels energy currents. Sedona and Egypt were the first of many playgrounds to explore.

In Drunvallo Melchizedek's book, *Serpent of Light*, he describes in detail his journey inside the great pyramid of Giza. He talks about his adventure down into the very bottom where a tunnel, termed the antechamber, leads to a sudden dead end.

He vividly shared his journey down that tunnel into the darkness to face all of his fear and allow it to leave him, and be cleared by the earth. This story stayed with me. Every word he described resonated in my body as one who had lived with fear on a continuous basis. If it were possible to leave my fear in the Great Pyramid of Giza, I would journey to any corner of it to do so.

The day of our private time in the pyramid arrived. Some of our group got really sick the night before and found themselves purging in preparation for their entrance. We were all excited and very centered at the same time. We entered and climbed, hunched over, up through narrow tunnels, first to the king's chamber.

Within the king's chamber is the much-talked-about sarcophagus, whose use has been widely speculated about. The group we were with believed it to be the chamber in which one would enter and travel through portals to other star systems. One would enter the sarcophagus, journey, and return three days later. The theory was that the stone vessel had also been moved from its original position.

Our group formed a circle along the outside edge of the chamber, and we connected our intention to a loving and unified source. Each of us took turns to lay down in the sarcophagus while John Dumas, a gifted shaman and didgeridoo player, activated the space by applying the healing sound currents of the didgeridoo to our bodies. His circular breath pattern created vibrations that met with the cells in our bodies, while Tiffany Tatum, a gifted vocal sound healer, sang out our names, tethering us to her voice.

This was a good thing, for when I lay my body down and repeated the phrase "Original position" three times in my head, I felt the sensation of shooting off into a space far away, and I could barely hear her voice in the distance.

We only got to spend a few moments in this position because our group was large and time was precious. I didn't have any sense of where or what the short journey was about, but it seemed that explanations for experiences in Egypt were irrelevant. We were just there to take them in through our cells. We were there to be reactivated.

The acoustics in the king's chamber was like nothing I experienced before. Tiffany continued to sing in the space long after the group began to spread out and explore further chambers and passages. She has one of those voices that has multiple octaves all at once. She has this loving and gentle ability to smile at you while she gently hip-checks you a little bit out of your comfort zone. In the years that followed, we became great friends.

My next stop and my pure determination were to enter the antechamber at the bottom of the pyramid. Together with my son, we led the charge to the bottom. He was determined to be the first into the passageway and I followed a few people behind him. It was narrow and interesting to ponder the knowledge that you were deep beneath the earth, under the Great Pyramid of Giza. What did that even mean? It was mind blowing.

We crawled until the end was reached. All the while, I expected my fears to rise up and accumulate into a distilled essence of offering, but instead, I felt a strong sense of courage. I took a few moments when we stopped to close my eyes and connect with my surroundings. I prayed to whatever benevolent energies were in the space to take from me any fear that limited my ability to move forward in my life, asking for it to be transmuted in this very chamber. Then I ceremoniously buried it in the pathway to be taken into the earth and cleansed. I felt at peace.

Egypt marked the start of a global travel call that had now been initiated, and soon France, Peru, Kauai, Costa Rica, and the Maya lands would call me in.

•

# Chapter 8

I flew direct from New York to Phoenix on our return to North America. My 200-Hour *Hatha* Yoga Teacher's Training was about to begin—thirty days of time all to myself, in Sedona, AZ, immersed in deep, energetic, and physical healing. I was excited.

I rented a condo near the studio and excitedly unlocked its door in anticipation of exploring my new space. As soon as I entered, I cried. The space was quite nice and absolutely fit all of my needs, but it felt empty, and that brought in the awareness that I was on my own for the first time since I was eighteen. Now I was forty-two. Except for a short couple of months in an apartment, I had never really lived on my own.

I turned around, walked out of the door, and headed for the grocery store. My new home needed supplies. Fresh food and flowers were added to incense and candles. I gathered it all from various shops and returned to create a space I could feel happy in.

I unpacked my portable iPod dock and blasted beautiful music into the space as I smudged with incense and lit candles. A nice, warm meal and the sound of my own voice began to fill the space with energy and relaxation. I unpacked and settled in. A whole new journey in my life was about to begin. I had no idea how significant that would prove to be.

Sraddhasagar is the owner and founder of 7 Centers Yoga Arts. She is a brilliant *yogini* whose diverse background and travels led her to many great teachers and practices around the world. In addition to embodying and living what she taught, Sraddha was able to transmit a depth of understanding that continues to blow my mind and leave me fully mesmerized by her words and the implications of everything she shares.

For example, in the 200-hour training I had just entered, Sraddha had us rise and walk in a circle, continuously moving about the room. Then, she would systematically instruct us to alter our posture and observe how it made us feel. First, we walked with our shoulders slumped forward, creating a curve in our back that looked as though we were protecting our hearts. Next, we walked with our chins jutted forward, as though attempting to have our heads scout ahead to what was coming next. After that, she had us raise our shoulders toward our ears, walk with toes pointed inward, and then with toes pointed outward.

Each variation of our posture created different energetics within our bodies. Literally, different energy pathways would be opened and others would be compressed. This created different thought patterns and emotions. As we folded inward upon ourselves, a sense of introversion would result; wide-open hips and feet made us extrovert. Her point was that our mind, emotions, and thoughts were connected to our body posture.

Not only would our patterns of thinking and feeling cause us to hold our bodies in certain ways, but our body being held in a certain way would lead to how we would think or feel. It was all a big cycle, which could be interrupted or altered from any or both approaches. Changing the way we thought and felt would result in a different posture, and changing our physical posture would change how we thought and felt. They were intrinsically connected.

She further asked for a volunteer to stand in the middle of the room to have their posture analyzed. I leapt at the chance. It was odd for me to put myself in the spotlight, but I was so excited by the idea that Yoga could affect how I would think and feel that I just wanted to dive in.

Sraddha began to describe the posture of my right foot. Across my toes were wrinkles, little lines running from edge to edge at each joint. She asked the group to observe how it appeared that my toes were gripping the earth. She was right. This posture indicated to her that I didn't feel safe, and so my body was literally trying to cling to the earth for connection. She further concluded that my thoughts and emotions would be both caused by and reinforced by this posture.

Next, she observed that my arches were quite flat to the floor. The bone structure was healthy, so it wasn't that I had collapsed arches, but the muscles were weak and indicated that I was one who felt the weight of the world on her shoulders. She followed the foot up to the ankle and noticed how it pronated outward to cause me to place more of my weight on the right hip than evenly on both. I relied more on the masculine action side of doing rather than the feminine receptive side of being.

More and more was described as the students gazed at me in sympathy for all that she was able to see was afflicting me. Sraddha picked up on their discomfort and reminded them that this was not me she was talking about; it was my mind. To Sraddha, the two were separate and distinct and should never be confused. For the rest of us, that was a theory yet to be grokked.

I was mesmerized by her every word. She described me perfectly, as though she had observed me my whole life. The way I saw it was that this woman had the keys to correcting me, and I was excited and willing to pour all of my effort into the task.

The Yoga training was an immersion. We would rise to begin practices at 4:30 a.m., gathering silently in the big room to be led through asana (Yogic postures), *pranayama* (breath techniques), mantra (sacred chants), and relaxation. The backbone of all of it was the back breathing that Mira had introduced me to in our sessions together.

Morning practice was followed by breakfast, a karma Yoga cleaning assignment in the center, and then deeper instruction into the philosophies of Yoga and the technical aspects of the asanas and other limbs of Yoga. Everything was reinforced by personal practice and further exploration of the effects of each within our own body and mind.

A hike into the red rocks fed into lunch and deep relaxation techniques. In the later afternoon, we explored anatomy and different styles of Yoga. This went on five days a week and included additional workshops and explorations on Saturdays. Sunday was our day to resupply and integrate our week.

Every day, the breath and the alignments, together with the sounds my own voice vibrating in my body, began to literally open me up. Tensions and constrictions that had been solidified within my very tissues, muscles, tendons, and fascia were beginning to release. As breath was brought deep into the body, space was being created and my movement range was increasing. Long *shavasanas* at the end of each practice gave my body the time to release all that had been invited to go. I felt sensations evaporate from the body like steam, along with emotions and thoughts.

Each day, I met with a new edge of fear and contraction and then literally held the space within the practice to allow it to just be. In that act of allowing, it would magically release. I still hear, to this day, the voice our *sadhana* teacher, Zac, as he would consistently repeat, "Just observe the thoughts and emotions that arise. No judgment, no aversion." Zac is an amazing example of Yoga in action.

Time was always set aside to share our experiences. This was an incredible time for me. I would sit and listen to each student share what had been going on for them in the practice. They would express with such honesty and vulnerability in a space that held no judgment for their confessions. I saw myself in all of their words and was healed by simply listening. Overall, I was pretty quiet in these circles and would feel a sense of panic as my turn approached. We were being trained to observe ourselves from an objective perspective. We were being trained to connect with our true aspect and see through her eyes.

Still in the habit to be what reflection would be most accepted, I feared that my sharings would seem dumb or irrelevant or even weird to the others. This was the hardest part of the training for me, as each day I was invited to just be authentic. I longed for the experience as much as I feared it.

The other aspect of the training that pushed my envelope was the *shatkarmas*. These are physical cleanses. I laugh now because I realize I have became so comfortable with them that often, when I talk about them, people get really squeamish. To me, they are so beneficial and natural that I forget how sensitive they can make people feel. I must include them in my story.

We began each day by dry brushing the body in a specific pattern. This removed dead skin cells as well as activated our lymphatic system to drain. The brushing was followed by a shower and an oil massage to feed the skin and activate the whole body. The massage was so nurturing and really moved my mind into realizing that I was allowed to start my day by taking care of myself.

A scraper was used to clean the tongue and remove any of the toxins that had risen to its surface during the night. By looking at the tongue, and observing the areas and color of the coating, one could map back to all of the organs of the body. These were Ayurvedic principles. Tooth brushing was followed by sesame oil and sea salt paste gum massage. Keeping the gums free of bacteria growth ensures healthy gums and teeth, but also keeps infections from running the meridians from the teeth all the way to different organs of the body. It also helps keep heart valves from being damaged by such bacteria found in the mouth.

Warm salt water was run through each nostril as we used a Neti Pot to clean the sinus cavity. This was really important to our practice. Each nostril feeds its opposite brain hemisphere with the *prana* from the breath. So when you inhale through the right nostril, you are feeding the left-brain, and inhaling through the left nostril feeds the right-brain. At any one time in the day, one can close off a nostril, check the flow of the inhale through the other, then switch and check the other side to compare which nostril is more open or dominant.

By observing the dominance of the nostril, you can determine which side of the brain is receiving more *prana* and, therefore, more active in the moment. Each side or hemisphere of the brain is responsible for different functions and ways of perceiving. The left brain is very masculine and linear in its processing. It is here that functions such and logical thinking and mathematics are performed. The right side is more abstract and feminine, a good place for conceptual processing and feeling into one's space.

When both nostrils are open and the breath is flowing to both hemispheres of the brain, the person is more balanced. Beginning our day this way literally helped us to stay more centered throughout the practices. This is also the logic behind *pranayama* exercises such as *Nadi Shodhana*, an alternate nostril breathing technique. In these, one can work with opening different aspects and balancing the mind.

The most challenging of the *shatkarmas* were the *Kunjali* and the *Laghoo Shankhaprakshalana*. Each practice involved drinking warm salt water first thing in the morning on an empty stomach. In *Kunjali*, one would drink a good liter and a half of warm salt water until the stomach was full. Then the practitioner would use a finger in the back of the throat to expel the water back out. This was a very challenging practice for many. While the action is the same as throwing up, the experience is quite different. It is more like washing a pot, sending the water in and then dumping it out.

With bulimia and the unpleasant emotions people have experienced when they feel sick and uncontrollable in the throes of purging this way, many have difficulty approaching this practice. I was lucky. In my pregnancy many years prior, I had a short bout of morning sickness and got really relaxed at just letting it go so I could get on with my day. *Kunjali* was an easy practice for me. The benefits are so far ranging from simply cleansing the upper digestive tract to the release of mucus from the lungs with the energy of upward movement in the expelling part of the practice. Fluid never enters the lungs, but the act of bringing it up invites the lungs to let go as well. Asthma sufferers often report great relief from this practice.

For me, the gift was in the release of emotions. All of my life, I had held fears, worries, and sadness in my tummy. This practice let the energies go and I began to deepen in my own comfort in the body.

The second of the salt-water practices was *Laghoo Shankhaprakshalana*. We only did this practice once. We would drink a couple of glasses of the warm salt water and then do a series of Yoga postures to move it through the digestive tract. Then drink a couple more glasses and repeat. This went on for three to four cycles. Once the salt water had made its way through the lower intestinal pathways, the urge to let it go would arise and one would spend the next little while on the toilet, experiencing the purge from the bottom end this time.

It would continue until clear water flushed through. It is a highly effective full digestive system cleanse.

Luckily for us, the studio chose a teacher to guide us who had experienced a profound healing in his first run with it. Not only did his body cleanse, but he was able to release deeply held emotions surrounding a family member who significantly affected his life. His name was

Jacob, and he actually made the practice fun. I know! How could this be fun?

Jacob picked the loudest, most energetic music to blast in the background. As we all stood near the warm pot of salt water, rounds of joyful toasts were initiated to raise the mood into one of a party. This helped with the fear that was surfacing as the mind was once again brought into a zone of discomfort and worry. The *asanas* done between our toasts were done with laughter and vigor, and the whole thing had the feel of celebration.

Jacob not only taught us how to properly execute the cleanse, but he taught us how one could make even the most squeamish of procedures pleasant. I was deeply grateful for all of the lessons I received that day. Something that seems so simple taught me to walk to the edge of cliffs and trust that I could handle the jump to the waters below. There were many more cliffs coming.

One day in our afternoon Yoga practice, Sraddha led us through a guided meditation. In it, she asked us to place our awareness at our eyebrow center as if we were looking through our third eyes. I had my eyes closed and I could see my body sitting upright, cross-legged with a face of effort, attempting to pull my focus to that part of the body, but I wasn't inside my body, so I couldn't actually do what she asked.

After the practice, as we shared, I revealed my experience and Sraddha instructed me to keep trying to get into my body with my awareness. Having my awareness outside of the body was a sign that I was once again not fully connecting. It was the discomfort I felt in physical form that kept me out. It was the fear of feeling and experiencing life through the form. I felt more comfortable simply hanging out beside my body. This was more evidence of my dissociation with my reality. The practices continued.

Twice a day for each of the days, we would be treated to the most delightful food. Mira, the young yogini master who had sparked my love of Yoga, was also the Ayurvedic chef. If Yoga transmissions were her gift, preparing food was her mastery. Mira poured love and the fascination of what each food did for our bodies into everything she created. Not only would we gather to offer loving intention to the food we were about to ingest, but we would receive a download about how each food affected us, physically and energetically. It was fascinating and yummy.

As the weeks continued and my knowledge grew, my body and mind began to shift dramatically. I was flexible with physical movement and had begun to observe myself in ways I had never known. I observed the feelings and thoughts arise within me only to simply observe how they affected me, not trying to change them or feel any further judgment of them. I was simply observing myself exactly where I was in each moment.

The breath deepened in my body and my diaphragm released long-held fears, I was becoming strong, lean, and supple in every way one can mean that. I was becoming relaxed in a way I had never known before. And aside from missing my boys, I was really happy and more so content.

One day, while lying in *shavasana* at the end of a practice, I suddenly realized that I was looking at my eyebrow center from inside my body. I was in my body! This felt new. As I fell into this awareness, I realized that I was crooked. My head was slightly tipped to the right side and I could feel my right shoulder and hip pulled toward one another, creating a whole curve in my body toward the right side, folding in on itself. This matched my physical posture exactly.

The day Sraddha began at my foot to provide an example of how the body and mind are connected, she did not stop at my foot. She traced my posture all the way up my body. I leaned to the right side, placing more weight on my right hip. I dropped the right shoulder and raised the left. My head tipped to the right but then tried to correct itself in how I held my neck and shoulders. The actual sphenoid bone, the one behind the eye sockets, was slightly crooked in my skull. All of this tipped and twisted my pelvis ever so slightly.

As I lay there on my mat, finally in my own body, I was totally connected with the energetic version of myself and she was literally crooked in the body. I slowly and delicately attempted to straighten myself out without moving a physical muscle. I simply connected with that energetic awareness and made tiny adjustments to its perspective. I felt energetic releases through the tissues of the body and the sensation of muscles relaxing as tiny points of awareness came into focus. I didn't want *shavasana* to end. I was in my body! Wow!

The training wound to an end and I completed the whole process, including the practicum at the end to receive my teaching certification. I still didn't feel I would teach, but it would be crazy not to achieve this mark after putting in all the time.

The truth was that I didn't feel I knew enough or had enough experience to share with others. My journey with

Yoga had literally just begun and I was sure it would prove the biggest gift of my life. I was steeping in gratitude and hope for a much different life to come.

The whole process had brought me into an experience of fully embodying the knowledge presented. The practices gave me personal contact with the connection between the body, mind, and soul in a way that was tangible and useful in my life. Simply picking one spot in the connection circuit to interrupt would allow me to break a pattern. Simply adjusting my spine to an upright position would allow my heart meridians to open and allow me to feel more comfortable and confident in my body. Simply extending my inhales and exhales would shift me into a relaxed nervous system response and allow racing thoughts to calm. It was that simple. It was obvious once you truly saw it. It was all connected.

Now, being in my body more than not gave me the practice of interacting with the world from the inside out instead of operating like a remote-controlled vehicle cruising through a room. I was in the driver's seat more than not, and while I still didn't have a full appreciation for what this meant, it was the perfect beginning. And everything has beginnings and layers. What a rich and magical design this experience of human life really is. It is complex and yet fundamental in the same moment. With multiple points of awareness for us to place our focus on, life is literally an infinite choice of potentials. Absolutely mind blowing.

# Chapter 9

Life resumed and, within a short period of time, I was back in many old patterns of tension and fear. Only this time, I had the memory of how that could feel different, so the pain of my reversion was more uncomfortable than before. They say ignorance is bliss, and now I knew what they intended by that saying.

It seemed that despite all of the training and practice, once I was in familiar territory, the same old triggers would fire within me and my behavior would revert. The only difference was that now I could see it while it was happening. The truth was that I could no longer NOT see it.

The year that followed included travel through Canada, a lot more reading, and a journey to France. The journey to France was my first long-distance journey on my own. I was meeting up with four other women to follow the path of Mary Magdalene and to connect with my ancient roots there. It was a short trip, but it was one that my inner self needed to give me in order to fully spark the wanderer spirit I had buried so deeply in my youth. I would be traveling the globe soon to touch many sacred sites, and France was my first after Egypt, and necessary to open that feminine aspect within. It was so nourishing.

Back with my partner, I found that I still longed to go back into the cocoon of 7 Centers and find that magical place within me again that I rested in during my *Hatha* training. Maybe I just didn't get it. Maybe I needed to do it again. At the time, I didn't realize that everything has layers and that my first month of training gave me the experience of clearing a lot from my body and mind, and it gave me tools and techniques to keep clearing myself. It also gave me lenses from which to view my own behavior so that I could begin to consciously make new choices for myself. Practice was going to be life long, but I still yearned to be fixed.

I quickly found a reason to return to 7 Centers when I discovered that a weeklong course was coming. It was a chakra intensive. Chakras are energy centers within the body that run along the spine. They are often referred to as wheels or vortexes because they spin.

In the body, there are many pathways that energy runs through, but in the spinal region, there are three major pathways. One is called *Ida* or the lunar channel. It runs from the base of the spine, spiraling upward to flow through the right hemisphere of the brain. It is considered feminine in nature. The second is *Pingala* or the solar channel. It spirals in the opposite direction through the left hemisphere of the brain. It is considered masculine.

Each time the two streams of energy meet, a chakra is created. Chakras are found in the same location as the major physical nerve plexus of the body. The channel that is flowing with more strength will determine the direction of the spin of each chakra and each chakra will alternate direction.

For example, if you were to lie on your back on the floor and I were to hold a pendulum over your heart center, the pendulum would begin to move. If your heart center were flowing energy in an open fashion, it would spin in a circle. When the feminine polarity is stronger in the moment, the heart spins clockwise, from my point of view. If the masculine polarity were stronger in the moment, it would spin in the opposite direction. From there, I could systematically move my pendulum above the locations of the other six major chakras, and each time I moved to the next chakra, the direction would reverse.

There is so much to share about chakras, but this is a basic introduction of the mechanics.

Along with the two polar channels spiraling, like the serpents found on the medical symbols we've all come to recognize, is the main channel, *shushumna*, which runs up the center of the spine. When Kundalini energy, a dormant potential energy residing at the base of the spine, awakens, it runs up this central channel.

I arrived back in Sedona by air this time, landing in Phoenix and driving up to Sedona in a rental car. I would only stay a short while this time. Still on my quest to heal and become comfortable in my body, I had planned to explore deeper and additional alternative healing modalities after the chakra intensive concluded. I had been looking at clinics in California that specialized in alternative modalities that worked directly with the brain itself. The little voice was guiding me again and I was listening intently as it whispered *"brain training."*

I stayed in the spare room of Tiffany's house. She is the vocal sound healer who tethered me to the sarcophagus in the Great Pyramid of Giza with her magical voice. She is also the one I went to France with. After a peaceful rest, I found myself in the shower under a cascade of warm water.

I love showers. Showers have always been my method of rinsing away the cobwebs from my thoughts and emotions, a literal cleanse on every level. The shower was also where I received a great deal of guidance from my little voice.

This particular morning, the voice was clear and succinct. *"Check the Creative Life Center calendar,"* was all it said. The Sedona Creative Life Center is a beautiful property off Schnebly Hill Road that is home to many sacred events and sharings. There is always something interesting occurring there, and it would be good to check out that night's offering because Tiffany had a gathering happening in her home and I wanted to give her privacy.

Up on my computer, the calendar popped and the sound of "uh-huh" reverberated through my cells before I could even make out the words that appeared. That night, Dr. Sung Lee of the Brain Well Center was speaking about Brain State Technologies Brain Optimization Training. This was it!

Dr. Lee, Sung, as he likes to be referred, is one of those souls who is simply beautiful and you can see it right away. There is a purity and a truth that simply is who he is on every level. You can feel that everything he does comes from a deeper core intention, and this intention is to help people. His wife, Angie, is the same.

The presentation flowed with information that fascinated me and answered all of the questions that the due diligence part of my mind was demanding. Sung shared how the founder of the technology, Lee Gerdes, was a computer algorithmic specialist responsible for such programming as the one found on Amazon Books, where you like one book and the system suggests another you may also like.

Mr. Gerdes was the victim of a brutal mugging in which he was beaten by four men. His physical wounds healed but he found himself in a state of posttraumatic stress that wasn't going away. He couldn't get comfortable and so he sought every alternative method of healing that he thought might assist.

In this quest, he found biofeedback training. This was giving him some success but not what he felt he was seeking, so he decided to pool his own computer programming knowledge with the biofeedback and create a real-time neuro-biofeedback system that would significantly help him retrain the responses within his own brain patterns. This was exactly what he did. Brain State Technologies was born and he was his first client. With the help of medical professionals, he created a model that is now serving many people through affiliate offices around the globe. Sung had opened an office in Sedona.

Sung explained that by placing electrodes on the scalp of the head, brain waves could be fed into a computer. The computer program would then feed the waves back to you through sound into the ears. The phenomena basically boiled down to the brain hearing itself and going, "Oh! That's me. Let me fix myself up." It was a technologically driven form of literal self-awareness.

Sung further explained that brain patterns within us could be in stuck mode. In the example of Lee Gerdes, the trauma he suffered left his brain stuck in fight/flight mode. This is a state when the sympathetic nervous system is switched on to send blood and nutrients to the muscles and lungs for fleeing or fighting the current danger. With his brain stuck in this pattern, Mr. Gerdes was in a constant state of high alert and unable to find relaxation. In addition, his body would have been in a steady flow of stress-response hormones. I'm sure you can imagine how uncomfortable that would be.

If he had not found relief, a certain course of longer-term consequences would have begun to unfold. By releasing this pattern within the brain and returning it to a normal state of equilibrium, Mr. Gerdes effectively altered the entire course of his coming life experiences.

Sung brought up a computer graphic model in which a line began to spiral on the screen. He described that this line represented the current course of our life, based on current neural pathways and tendencies. Then he suggested that we look at what would happen if we altered that by even a five percent improvement in brain balance and optimization. A second line representing this began to run alongside the current line. At first, they pretty much followed the same course, but soon, the second line was beginning to chart a different course. We could see that the life would be altered.

Next, Sung suggested we look at fifty percent improvement, and again, the model was started. This time, the line representing the new pattern pulled away from the existing life line and showed a significant difference right away. This was what I was after and I was really excited now. Saying yes to this training was a no-brainer, pun intended.

The presentation ended and I made my arrangements. First, I would do the chakra intensive and then the brain training. I felt such a surge of hope. Deep inside, I knew that this would be significant.

The chakra intensive began the next morning with early morning *sadhana* practice, as usual. Quiet, dimmed lighting, internal focus through breathing and meditation. It felt so good to be back within the container of transformation that felt as much like a womb as it did a studio.

The practices were intense. This was Kundalini Tantra Yoga. We were placed in postures for longer periods of time, anywhere from six to twenty-two minutes. As we held these postures, we focused our awareness to visualizing color within the region of the chakra we were working with that day. We also mentally vibrated mantras to attune the energy of that center to a balanced and open flow.

All the while, physical, mental, and emotional sensations would arise. The body would burn or tingle, thoughts would come up, and emotions would bubble. We would just follow our breath, see the color, and chant the *Bija* Seed Mantra over and over in our heads. The time would pass and soon we would be set free of the posture. The practice was simply to stay in it as long as one could. Some of this was very challenging.

If one were able to keep the mind neutral in the observer position, he or she would find the energy building and pathways being cleared. If the mind began to race, the sensations would intensify and the student would often end up moving out of the posture to then reset and begin again. I held steady.

As I held the postures, despite the intensity, many things would happen. I would sweat, feel panic rise and move through me, tears would sometimes erupt and flow down my cheeks. In one of the practices, the heart chakra specifically, my whole body started to shake, inviting release from deep within my tissues. All one had to do was watch and breathe, chant and visualize, and years of repressed experience and stuck energy would be lifted for release.

Once the timer sounded and we were released from our hold, we would surrender into a long *shavasana* and experience the run of energy as it poured though the now opened pathways. We would literally expand beyond the borders of our skin and out to infinity, all the while perfectly anchored in the core of our body. This was my practice! I had found my lifelong tool.

Later, we learned that by compressing and applying tension to the muscles and connective tissues of the body, we were, in effect, accessing the crystalline structure in which it was made of. Silica is a base ingredient in collagen found within our connective tissue, and connective tissue makes up much of the body.

As we applied the pressure to this structure, we would back up energy and build it; we would squeeze blood from organs, preparing them for a fresh surge of new blood to come in. All the while, we would use our visualization and inner voice to build a frequency from sound and color to attune the energy to a specific harmonic. This harmonic would match the frequency of the chakra itself. Once the process of building, pooling, and squeezing the area was complete, we would release the energy and the flows to flood through the area, sweeping away any contracted blockages from the crystalline structures of the silica. This is profound and deeply effective work.

Done within the container of an intensive training, the practitioner is safely held in a space of healing and is given the opportunity to be supported in the sharing of the group. These practices bring deeply seeded issues to the surface to be looked at and cleared. This work raises your consciousness to a whole new level, as the energy clears and activates the centers.

Kundalini Yoga, and specifically the chakra work, was about to become a significant part of both my healing and what I would share. This was my first taste of the tantra practice.

After a week of this intensive, I was like a freshly wrung-out and laundered cloth—bright, fresh, and clean. Next was brain training.

# Chapter 10

My sessions began with a long questionnaire and a brain map. The questionnaire asked for medical information and to describe what my intentions for the training were. This was to help align the training with my goals. The brain map was to get an idea of what my brain was doing in the current moment.

Electrodes were placed on my head in various locations to pick up the signals from different parts of my brain. Then I was asked to do various tasks, from reading, to math calculations, to visualizations of color and images. All of this data collected to form a picture of what was happening with my brain.

The picture revealed several things. First, the balance between right and left hemispheres was good, but the balance between the front and back was off. I had more activity in the back brain, the reptilian brain, which indicated that I was stuck in a sympathetic freeze mode. I was in fight/flight most of the time.

Further examination revealed that the blow I had received to the back of the head during my car accident was contributing to this. This and the current state of the tensions in my marriage.

Next, it was shared that a parasympathetic freeze mode was also discovered. This was believed to be a pattern established at about the age of five, when some experience would have been too much for my mind to endure. Because it was deemed too stressful by my mind, I reacted like a deer in the headlights, and instead of fighting or fleeing, I froze. In these situations, one often represses the memory and moves on. Here was my proof.

Sung took great care in ensuring I understood that the training would likely bring the buried emotions to the surface to be released, and that they may rise along with whatever the memories were. He wanted me to understand that this process may be uncomfortable. The upside would be the release of this set pattern of reaction and that I would soon be able to feel my emotions in ways I had not been able to since that young age. In truth, I had no way of understanding what he meant.

I sat listening to this assessment and felt sure that it was accurate. Here was the proof I needed that my recovered memories, which had surfaced two years prior, were likely real. And now, I was sitting in a chair that could literally cleanse the experience from my body and from my autopilot reaction system. We could not start fast enough.

The first session began. Protocols were set up in the computer, electrodes were placed on my scalp, and earbuds were installed in my ears. My first task was to watch a bar on the computer screen and attempt to use my state of inner relaxation to bring the bar downward on the screen. As the brain waves were fed into the computer, the sound of a xylophone being played returned in my ears. This was a representation of my brain waves coming right back in for my brain to observe.

The first exercise lasted for about ten minutes, and then the electrodes were moved and a new set began with a new task. This continued in short cycles as I moved through visualizing shapes and colors, imagining a walk in a forest, being in my favorite place in nature, and peeling the aspects of myself away like an onion. Sometimes, my eyes were open and I was reading; sometimes, I was deep in a visualization as I imagined my brain being washed in a shower of light. I loved my sessions.

The first four two-hour appointments sent my brain deeper into a parasympathetic freeze mode. Somewhere in me was the urge to protect me from the suppressed area at all costs, but the persistence of the training paid off when, in the fifth session, the barrel of toxic emotions was cracked open.

It literally felt like this to me. Suddenly, I felt a sense of panic flood through my whole body, and by the time I could say the word panic, it had switched to sadness, then fear, then terror, and so on. Each intense emotion moved through me like a wave, and I used all of my Yogic training to just sit and observe the sensation and breathe.

At one point in my meditation, I found myself on a beach. I could hear the waves crashing against the shore and feel the moist sand beneath my knees as I sat on them with my forehead to the earth. I imagined that barrel of toxic emotions, with its lid pried open, pouring its liquid contents into the earth. Mother earth was welcoming the release and instantaneously transmuting it back into healthy, vibrant energy. I was letting it all go.

No actual memories came with it, but the feelings were the most intense I had experienced; yet they just flowed out effortlessly. Later that day, when the training ended, I wandered into the backyard at the home I was staying in and placed my forehead to the earth. I sat and breathed like that for an hour, asking the red earth to cleanse me.

I welcomed the visualizations where light showered my brain as I continued through the whole set of ten sessions. I was literally cleaning my brain and all of its dysfunctional patterns of being. Most importantly, I already felt different.

All of my life, I had operated like one with both the gas and the brakes on all the time. I remembered literally finding my toes gripping the bottom of my shoes, as I would drive to work first thing in the morning. I would already be tense inside my body, poised and ready to jump at the drop of a pin.

In this way of being, I was always managing a continuous cycle of thoughts and sensations. A thought of fear would arise and my body would tense. The tension in the body would drive the next thought and that thought to the next tension. It would begin to loop until it ran its course. Sometimes, the thought would initiate the cycle, but sometimes, a physical sensation would start it, like walking into a room of people and feeling that wham in the solar plexus for no apparent reason. I had lived my life this way for as long as I could remember, in a continuously managed state of fear.

This cycle was broken now. That deserves repeating. This cycle was broken! I could have a thought but not experience the resulting physical contraction. The physical sensation no longer grasped for a thought to explain it. I was calm and this calm was real.

Within this new state of peace was a clarity and sharpness in my awareness. No longer taxed by the constant flow of thoughts and sensations, I could see beyond myself into the big world around me and began to experience it on a whole new level.

I left the eighth session, jumped into my rental car, and headed into Oak Creek Canyon for an afternoon drive. The canyon road winds through overhanging trees in a beautiful, red rock setting. It is an invigorating drive with speed limits of forty miles per hour. I headed up the road completely relaxed, reaching speeds in excess of sixty, as though I was sitting on a couch, watching a movie. The alert and relaxed state of my mind not only was able to navigate the road at high speeds, but was catching the visuals of butterflies' wings as they flapped by the side of the road. This was an incredibly heightened state of awareness. It was a whole new experience and I liked it a lot!

By the end of the tenth session, I felt brand new. I eagerly asked Sung to show me what percentage of improvement I had made. I self-assessed and hoped that it would be at least thirty percent, so I could know that my life course would be significantly altered. He looked at me, pulled a comparative of start and finish sessions up onto the screen, and said, "Angela..." and then he paused for my attention, "you had a 600 percent improvement in brain balance."

Six Hundred percent echoed in my mind. My whole life just changed and absolutely anything was possible now.

I headed for Canada. All of these years, my relationship had been difficult and, in large part, it was because I was in a constant state of fear. How had this affected things? Now that I had broken this pattern and the fear was gone, what magical things could shift for us? I was really excited to get home and share all of this experience with him. I felt a sense of hope that we could turn it all around.

It took only a week. My return and new state of being set off a bomb within our relationship that left me standing to the side, trying to understand what had just happened. I was different and now I could see clearly that the only answer was to leave. It had always been coming and was a necessary step in our evolution, but I was too afraid to see it. Now the fear was gone, or at the very least, it had shifted.

My very wise sister, Corinne, said it perfectly when she held me in her arms on the night I arrived at her doorstep in tears, suitcase hanging from my fingers. "Oh, Angela," she said, "Change happens when the fear of the unknown becomes less than the fear of staying the same. You can do this." She was bang on.

The steps that followed in getting accustomed to my decision to separate were difficult. I loved this man and deeply wanted him to be happy. We had been together for many years and I was very attached to him in every way. I had to actually sit and write down all of the reasons why I left him, for after a night's sleep, I would rise having forgotten them all.

Sung had cautioned me that because I had suppressed all of the memories and emotions, I had learned at a very early age to dissociate from my emotions. He said that once the brain pattern was released, I would begin to feel things in a way I had not experienced before, and that this would both be richer in my life experience but may come with a flood of release.

Then one morning, I was waking still lucidly in the early morning dream. I was on a large ocean ship and it was my job to watch a big door at the bottom of the ship. My shift was about to start and so I skipped my way down a flight of stairs, happy and joyful, en route to my post. As I rounded the last curve in the stairs, the door I was responsible for came into my vision. To my horror, I could see that the door had been pried back, as though a giant pop bottle opener had been applied to its edges.

I gasped and heard myself say, "Oh, no! Here comes the water!" And then my little voice said, *"No, here come the emotions."* I woke in an explosion of tears and loud sobs at 7:00 a.m. I cried nonstop until three that afternoon, when I found myself in a bathtub of warm water, listening to the littlest girl voice come out of my lips, saying, "Why don't they just love me the way I am?" And then the flood of tears stopped and I collapsed back into bed. I was fully surrendered to my own heart and relaxed to the core.

# Chapter 11

The time to step forward in my life, on my own, had arrived with the New Year, and the little voice wasted no time in making my plans. First, I would return to 7 Centers Yoga Arts in Sedona for the thirty-day Kundalini Yoga Teachers' Training in April. Second, I would head for Peru in September. This was going to be a full year and many more things were to be added as I was now escalated onto my solo path of self-realization.

Peru had been calling me since my experience with Wanda in the Medical Intuitive Training class a year and a half before. When she pulled the etheric little plate that covered my third eye, she awakened the knowledge that Peru would be significant in my life. Although it called me, I had no idea why.

I had long since found the group I would journey with, but their trip was always booked so far in advance that by the time I contacted them, they would be full. The universe was waiting for the perfect moment for me to go, so as soon as the prompting returned, I called them and booked my space.

A long drive down to Arizona for the Kundalini training was my next adventure. I excitedly made all of the arrival plans for accommodations, another condo in the exact same complex as my first Yoga training in Sedona. I booked massage therapy sessions and additional brain training sessions to deepen my clarity and functioning while preparing my body for the intensive. My life was opening to a brand-new page. I was both excited to go and sad to leave my family at the same time. It was always the wide spectrum of duality for me. I felt everything at once my whole life.

The Kundalini teacher, who was leading the course, was Hari Jap, a man who had been practicing Kundalini Yoga for thirty years. Hari Jap owns a studio in Phoenix called the Center for Divine Awakening and has a rich history within the Yogi Bhajan community of teachings.

As a young boy, Hari Jap had surgery to stabilize his spine, and in the procedure, metal rods were installed into his back to keep everything in proper alignment. This was followed by months of bed rest and healing. He was told by his medical team that he wouldn't be able to do most normal physical activities, but he didn't let their words sink in. Instead, he passed the time watching Kung Fu movies and began to plan his movement into the martial arts.

Martial arts led him to a Kundalini Yoga class and he settled into what was to be his practice and calling, and a life free of limitation. Hari Jap is one of the most egoless people I know. He is humble and purely grateful to be a vessel that is open to truth. He is constantly directing his students to look within themselves for their inner teacher as he diligently serves their highest aspect. He is a disciplined example of Kundalini Yoga in action.

I had been introduced to Kundalini back in the 200-Hour *Hatha* Program when Hari Jap would journey from Phoenix to Sedona each Wednesday evening for class. He would sit up on his white blanket on the stage and powerfully direct us through a *kriya*. The word *kriya* means complete action, and it is comprised of a series of exercises, done in specific order and time intervals. Each *kriya*, in its entirety, has a specific effect on the body, mind, and soul. The *kriyas* he taught had been shared by Yogi Bhajan and were maintained in practices all over the world.

Yogi Bhajan became a master of *Hatha* and Kundalini Yoga in his teenage years. He grew up in India and then followed his path to North America, when he received divine guidance to begin sharing the technology and practice with the Western world. Yogi Bhajan could see the nature of the times coming and he knew that people would need to strengthen their nervous systems and mental faculties to navigate what they would face. This is the exact time he was referring to.

He arrived in Eastern Canada and then made his way south into the US, spending time in New York and California, and later settling in Espanola, New Mexico, where a center and gathering grounds were created. He formed the 3HO Foundation; 3HO stands for Happy, Healthy, and Holy. Yogi Bhajan has now left his physical body but continues to inspire through the energy held in his subtle body. Kundalini Yoga, as taught by Yogi Bhajan, is shared worldwide.

Yogi Bhajan saw that the activations the practices brought required a solid structure of lifestyle to support them, so he paired his teaching with the habits and lifestyle of the Sikh community. One did not need to become a Sikh to practice or be taught, but the lifestyle of vegetarian diet, allowing the hair to grow and covering the head, among other aspects, were beneficial to receptivity, containment, and maintenance of the energy and the electromagnetic field of the body.

Schools certified by the Kundalini Research Institute offer teacher trainings worldwide, where one may attend and focus on this style of Kundalini Yoga.

I felt very lucky to be receiving instruction from Hari Jap and the 3HO lineage through 7 Centers Yoga Arts. I felt even more fortunate that the training was combined with other Kundalini lineages, such as teachings from *Swami Satyananda Saraswati* and the *Bihar* traditions of India, and *Vikashananda* of Nepal.

The usual ritual of early morning *sadhana* practice was once again how we began our day. This time, we would arrive, do a 3HO Yogi Bhajan *kriya*, and then chant for one hour. I could share a whole book on this practice known as Aquarian Sadhana. It is profound and leaves one in a beautiful state of bliss.

Kundalini Yoga is considered in the Yogi Bhajan traditions to be a Raja or royal Yoga. In the *Bihar* tradition, Tantra is considered the Raja Yoga and Kundalini Yoga falls under its umbrella.

In ancient Sanskrit language, "*tan*" means expansion and "*tra*" means liberation. Tantra is the expansion of consciousness and liberation of energy. It can also be defined as union of the polarities.

Many people think of Tantra and immediately go to the sexual practices known as Red Tantra. These are specific practices used by a couple to unify the sexual energy and direct it for the expansion of consciousness. There are also other practices such as Black Tantra, which uses the sexual energy of Red Tantra for deliberate manifestation effects in the outer world.

White Tantra, which is shared in more detail later in the book, is a practice involving partners who run energy circuits during long meditations, without the sexual component.

Essentially, Tantra is an umbrella under which many practices fall that bring about the awakening of one's consciousness and the liberation of energy into creative aspects. Within the essence of Tantra are lenses and practices that help us understand and experience our true self entering physical form, to create in a reality of three dimension. It is incredibly complex yet ultimately simple all at the same time. What we manifest all boils down to our frequency. That frequency gets expressed through the sound current (mantra) in the very vibrations of our thoughts, emotions, intentions, and words. This frequency interacts with the infinite energy potential of the void *(shuniya)* and its primal and sacred geometrical form (*yantra*) to create the blueprints for what we will birth. Living our true potential boils down to the clarity of the true self frequency making its way through the body system.

Kundalini Yoga is a science and technology that helps you open your channel, tune in to your true self, and align with your highest aspect. In that regard, it is most definitely a royal Yoga.

In my 200-Hour *Hatha* Yoga training, each Wednesday evening was met with excitement as Hari Jap arrived to teach. From my first class, I knew that Kundalini was my Yoga. Every movement combined with coordinated breath brought sensations of energy flowing through my body. It was palpable and invigorating, like the experience I had on Wanda's table on my first visit to Sedona. All of the Yoga practices I had done were so beneficial to my body and my mind, but Kundalini was something very special to me and called me in like the serpent charming its own master.

In Kundalini Yoga practices, several breath patterns are used, but two are predominant. The first is long, deep breathing. One inhales deeply, and the chest expands as the lungs fill. The diaphragm, the muscle that lies beneath the lungs, drops, extending the belly outward. On the exhale, the diaphragm rises as the lungs collapse and the belly moves inward. One takes long, slow, deep inhales, expanding the body in all directions and then releasing all of the air as the belly moves toward the spine. This is called diaphragmatic breathing.

Many people breathe in the chest or upper chest only and develop tightness in the muscles of the diaphragm, just below the rib cage. The diaphragm is the place in the body where we store tightly held fears. Conscious practice of long, deep breathing helps to release the tension and the contracted fears that are stored in this muscle tissue, to allow for deeper inhalation and more oxygen and energy to reach the body.

The second breath that is most commonly used in these sets is called breath of fire. Other traditions have the same or similar variations, such as *bhastrika* or *kapalabhati* breath. In this breath, one literally moves the diapragm like a bellows, the instrument used to fan a fire.

The easiest way to learn breath of fire is to sit comfortably, stick your tongue out, and begin to pant like a dog. Place one hand on the belly and notice that the belly is rapidly moving in and out with the breath. On the exhale, the belly moves in, and on the inhale, the belly moves out. Essentially, what you are doing is pumping the belly with the breath. In breath of fire, one does the same action, but instead of inhaling and exhaling through an open mouth, one inhales and exhales through the nose.

To train ourselves, we consciously pull the navel in on each exhale. By maintaining our focus on the exhale only, each time we relax the belly, the inhale simply happens naturally. If one focuses on both the exhale and the inhale, the tendency is to hyperventilate. If any discomfort arises, the practitioner is encouraged to simply stop, breathe normally, and begin again when ready.

All *pranayam*, or breath work, is done with a completely relaxed mind. One day, a practitioner may have a rapid breath of fire and the next may have to go really slow. The important part is to stay relaxed and breathe diaphragmatically.

When we breathe, we not only bring fresh oxygen to the lungs and expel carbon dioxide, we also bring in *prana*. *Prana* is the rejuvenating and healing life force energy. As *prana* is brought into the body, it enters the cerebral spinal fluid and excites it. The excitation occurs as the *prana* moves to the solar plexus region of the body, just below the belly button, and mixes with another energy known as *apana*. *Apana* is the eliminating energy of the body and it moves from the navel center to the base of the spine as the force that drives elimination.

When the two energies mix in the navel center, they create the necessary alchemical reaction to spark Kundalini to rise. Kundalini energy is said to be the dormant force that resides at the base of the spine in the root chakra, *Muladhara*. This chakra is located at the perineum for men, between the anus and the genitals, and at the cervix for women.

In Kundalini Yoga practices, as the *prana* and *apana* mix, one squeezes and lifts the muscles of the pelvic floor to draw the energy down to the root. This sparks the Kundalini to rise.

That explains the mechanics of activating the energy. Put more simply, we inhale and consciously direct and mix the flows of energy to awaken Kundalini and transform our consciousness.

Kundalini, which literally means the curl of the hair of the beloved, then rises in a three and one half spiral through the chakras to activate them and awaken the corresponding centers of the brain. This is how consciousness is raised. In all spiritual awakenings, Kundalini is the force that is present. That warrants repeating. In every spiritual awakening, Kundalini energy is present.

There are many opinions to the raising of Kundalini within the body. Most of us have heard the stories of dramatic sudden awakenings in which the spine feels like it's on fire, and one suddenly sees and experiences beyond the veils of typical reality. These are rare occurrences and generally result from blockages in the body being confronted by a sudden triggering of the energy.

Other opinions and my own experience share a variation of that, which is a much gentler experience of the energy. Kundalini is being activated all of the time in small spurts, and as Yogi Bhajan would say, "It's not hard to raise the energy; it's hard to keep it up."

The *kriyas*, as taught by Yogi Bhajan, are not specifically intended to raise the Kundalini in a public class, but more so are intended to prepare the body. Through consistent practice, the nervous system and glandular systems of the body are strengthened and prepared to run the energy. Pathways are cleared, chakras are cleared and aligned, and one's consciousness is evolved at a rate that is easier for the mind to integrate. When the energy rises suddenly and powerfully, the mind has a more challenging task to integrate the elevation.

My personal experience is a variation of many rates and ranges of intensity. My first was when I was on Wanda's table years before, when the breath activated the energy within my body and pushed against the blockages. The pathways in my body opened to a force that ran right through me. It was a power and spirit of its own. I lay in awe as I felt the sensations pour through every cell. The temperature was neither hot nor cold, but simply electric. The experience was accompanied by deep understandings and awarenesses that elevated my consciousness. There was nothing painful about it once my body let go of the blockage.

Many more experiences have followed, each with its own unique flavor and intensity. I am so far from the same person I was before Kundalini awakened and after. Different in the sense that I am increasingly becoming more authentic. By authentic, I mean that I am embodying my true self.

Back in the morning *sadhana*, we would perform the exercises within the *kriya* and mechanically move the energy within the spine through movement, breath, and *bandhas. Bandhas* are body locks. As described earlier, the root lock, or *Mulbandh*, is where we squeeze the muscles of the pelvic floor, lift and pull the navel in to direct the mixed *prana* and *apana* energy to the root center, to spark the Kundalini. This then moves the energy up the spine.

The second lock or *bandha* is the diaphragm lock or *Uddiyana Bandh*. This one asks us to pull the navel center in as we lift the muscles up under the ribs. It's a sucking in and up motion. This lock automatically forces a root lock with it. The third is the neck lock or *jalandhara bandh*. It is when the chin is brought toward the chest. It may be required to pull the chin all the way to the body or, most often, it is a light neck lock in which the back of the neck is simply brought straight. All three locks pulled together is called a *Mahabandh*, the great lock.

By systematically working the locks at the prescribed moment with *prana* and *apana* mixing, we hydraulically bring the energy up the spine. This helps to clear the chakra system and blockages in the body. As the energy spreads and cascades from the spinal vortexes known as chakras, it runs across the nerve plexus found at each center and clears the pathways. This strengthens the whole body and relaxes the glandular and hormonal systems, bringing them back into balance.

All of this physical stabilization allows the mind patterns to settle and release from habitual imbalance caused from high stress of modern life. Kundalini Yoga heals and allows us to be strong in handling anything that comes our way.

In our practice, we would breathe and move in specific ways to open the spine, move the energy, clear the pathways, and all of this would result in the sensation of energy pouring through the body. Then we would add mantra. Mantra was like a beautiful curl of decadent chocolate placed on top of a light and creamy mousse. I'm a Taurus who loves pleasure, In case you haven't figured that out.

Getting used to the chanting was interesting. At first, the mind questions the resemblance of a cult-like atmosphere. I kept getting visions of my father looking in the door, me all dressed in white, chanting. It made me giggle. Second, I was uncomfortable with the sound of my own voice. Somehow, in my early days of programming, a comment made by teenage friends about my nasally sound stopped me from expressing in public.

I would even mouth the words to "Happy Birthday to You" when forced to participate in the ritual. My close family heard me at times, but for the most part, I kept my singing to myself. The chants we worked with could be sung. Each day as we repeated the same seven in sequence, I would get more comfortable with my own sound and then began to explore its journey within my mouth.

Where would it bounce, curve, swirl, and vibrate? That allowed my awareness to travel with the sound into all of my cells, witnessing the exploration and the discoveries of density. The sound waves would bounce against an energy block like sonar finding a coral reef in the ocean, and then it would continue to vibrate like a jackhammer against cement. Most times, it was gentler than that and more like the sonic plaque remover at the dental office.

Any way you chose to look at it, the sound current was clearing away density and opening the pathways more and more each moment. I loved the morning chants. Each morning I was in such a state of bliss. The sound current itself was powerful, but the mantra, chanted in Gurmukhi, a Sanskrit-originated language, captured the outcome in the sound itself. For example, *Sat Nam*, pronounced "sut nom," translates to "truth is my identity" and, when chanted, vibrates to bring in your true self.

As manta is repetitively chanted, with clear enunciation, the tongue strikes the upper pallet of the mouth like fingers on a piano keyboard. The effect on the roof of the mouth sends waves and currents right into the cerebral brain fluid, affecting states of brainwaves and creating states of bliss.

In a sharing circle one morning, in my state of bliss after chanting for one hour, I alerted the group that I would be letting my voice rip from that point forward. I had such fascination with how it was changing my whole body and allowing me to express more authentically. They giggled as I demonstrated potential wavering and crackling of my voice that they may need to endure. I kept my promise and they did hear the crackling as I bravely let the apprehension and fear of expression get blown out with the force of my vibrating voice. Each time, I would simply let go of the need to sound perfect, the vibrations would blast through some contracted and contorted pathway, clearing and purifying my whole sound. The mantra is profound!

Sound was revealing its laser-like simplicity within the practice. This was only the tip of understanding. When one followed that into its more base form of frequency, one could easily see that frequency was present in all forms of energy. From the densest of the earth element to the lightest of ether, it is all frequency. Every thought, every emotion, every morsel of food ingested, and ultimately, the most powerful, every word spoken silently or aloud is frequency.

No wonder we could create our own reality. We were literal frequency being shot through a physical tube of alignment, set in the course of a specific attitude, through a holographic projection lens, and into the void of infinite potential.

The clearer and more finely tuned the adjustment and attitude of the lens, the more precise the creation could consciously be. The more the channel was cleared and tuned to my true self, the greater the potential of expressing my authentic purpose. Kundalini is my practice!

Thirty days of movement, breath, sound, and intention brought more rushes of energy up the spine, releases of emotions, tensions, and awarenesses that elevated me in my understanding of truth. I was not only in my body fully, I was expanding outward to infinity while securely anchored to my core.

The core piece of it all was the understanding of the three minds as is represented by this model. In 3HO Kundalini, they see us as having three minds—Negative, Positive, and Neutral.

Negative Mind's chief job is to contain our expansive self in physical form. Its very nature is contractive. It assesses risk and danger, and looks to keep us in good health.

Positive Mind's chief job is to express us through the form. Its very nature is expansion. It looks for opportunity.

When Negative Mind is out of balance, it goes into fear and over contraction, which can result in anxiety, paranoia or even physical densities and forms. When Positive Mind is out of balance, it goes into overexpansion and seeks cravings, which can result in compulsive behavior and addiction.

Both the Negative and Positive Minds are part of the body's autopilot system. They run off a database of impressions that are accumulated through the sensory perceptions of our experiences in life. The database is a storehouse of every single impression, whether we are conscious of it or not. In fact, most traditions believe that it also contains the impressions of every other lifetime lived.

From this database, as a new impression comes in, the Negative and Positive minds perform instantaneous searches to determine what the appropriate reaction would be. All of this is based on prior experience.

Then there is Neutral Mind. This is who we truly are. This is our true essence coming into the body. This is the little voice in my head. Neutral Mind operates as a response system, taking approximately nine seconds to review the autopilot reactions of the Negative and Positive Minds and then choosing a response that is Neutral and balanced, a choice that considers the higher potential, free of judgment.

The Neutral is the platform from which the practice continues, for whatever arises in the moment from the depths of the subconscious is then met with neutrality. In this neutrality, the experience is not held in the body or allowed to be reacted upon, but is instead simply observed and released. This is how you clear and hold space for yourself and others. This is the key to the whole practice of life.

I had found my zero point in the neutral mind and was able to hold the wide polarity of the full spectrum of my experiences at once. Free of judgment and aversion in many moments enabled me to let go of limiting beliefs and patterns that didn't serve the path ahead.

During the training, Hari Jap also prepared a Numerology Report on my birth date. The 3HO Kundalini tradition views the human as having ten different bodies. They are the soul; then the three minds, being the negative, positive, and neutral mind; the physical body; arc line, which is the halo that runs from ear tip to ear tip like a cap on the head, and also from nipple to nipple for a woman; the aura or electromagnetic field around the body; the *pranic* or breath body; the subtle body, which is said to carry the soul after physical death; and the radiant body.

By using five different calculations from the birth information, this system comes up with five numbers to correspond with the ten bodies. Two of these numbers represent challenges and are known as the soul number and karma number. The other three represent the gift, destiny, and path.

It is possible to also have an eleventh body. The eleventh refers to the full integration of all ten bodies as a mastery and command of all.

The numbers of my reading made a lot of sense to the way I had experienced my life. My challenge was the neutral mind, the fourth body. All of my life, I sought to find my center amongst the wild swings, from negative to positive, and sometimes both at once.

My arc line also presented a challenge, the sixth body, as I was easily rattled by outward projection and could easily go into stress response. Simply placing a head covering over the arc line helps to center me in times of stress.

These two challenging numbers really represented how I dealt with both my inner and outer worlds. My inner soul essence is that of a person at prayer, intuitive and coming from the arc line nucleus of the aura. When I feel disconnected from my soul, I lack trust of my intuition and become easily rattled and off center.

The way I dealt with the outside world was represented in my karma number, and in that case, the neutral mind. My challenge was to stay neutral in all situations, but when in the wide swings of the polarities, I would try to grasp for absolutes, believing that if I could control my outward circumstances, I would find balance. This resulted in forming a lot of opinions about others and myself.

The destiny number is representative of what you had spent lifetimes working on and of how other people saw you. Mine was the positive mind, body number three. People saw me as generally positive, as I tended to look for the silver lining in everything and would emphasize it.

My path number was also the neutral mind, which made so much sense. In my quest to manage my challenge, I was on my path.

The path of Neutral Mind was that of holding the cup of prayer. Holding the neutral space of pure, unconditional love and acceptance is the most healing feeling to me. Holding this for others is most definitely my path. Within this space of centered, zero point perspective is pure healing. For one who's life has oscillated in wild swings from opposing polarity; the neutral zero point is heaven.

My gift is the eleventh body, which is the full command of all ten bodies, and as I continue on my spiritual path, this gift will continue to reveal itself. This gift enables one to radiate from the zero point and hold an even more nurturing field for self and others. I feel very grateful for this life and opportunity to serve in this capacity.

The Tantra side of the Kundalini training focuses on teachings from Swami *Satyananda Saraswati* and is more deliberately focused on clearing and awakening chakras for the elevation of Kundalini energy and the raising of consciousness.

These practices are deep, focused, and highly effective. In the training, Sraddhasagar merged practices from both the *Satyananda* lineage and the *Vikashananda* teachings to create a practice-based experience.

They are best taught in an immersion format rather than a public drop-in setting, as the conditions that surface as a result of such training require a container to support the student.

This practice resonates within in me like an awakened memory, and my experience of each chakra continues to deepen in understanding and context. There is so much to share about the etheric anatomy of our avatar forms, and having a structure to frame one's experience of the energy helps the mind to integrate the flow.

It all starts with the spine. There are multiple pathways within the body that channel energy and, as described earlier, three main ones run up and down the spine. The first is known as *Ida*, the lunar channel. It begins at the base of the spine and spirals upward, passing through the center of the brain to feed the right hemisphere. The second one is called *Pingala*, the solar channel. It spirals in the opposite direction, through the left hemisphere of the brain.

Each time these two channels intersect, a major chakra is formed. Within the space of the spinal region, there are six main chakras, and a seventh, which is at the crown of the head. Chakras are known as wheels or vortexes because they spiral energy.

The direction of spin at each chakra alternates. For example, if we begin at the base of the spine at the first chakra, and this chakra spins clockwise, then the second center will spin counterclockwise, followed by the third center again spinning clockwise, and so on, alternating directions all the way up.

What determines the direction of each chakra is based on which of the two main channels is flowing more predominantly. If you were to lie down on the floor and I was to stand above you with a pendulum, I would be able to witness the spin of the chakra by the way it affected the pendulum. Holding the pendulum above an open heart center of an *Ida*-dominant flow would result in the pendulum spinning clockwise from my perspective. In a *Pingala*-dominant flow, it would spin counterclockwise.

*Ida* is associated with lunar feminine energy and *Pingala* is associated with the solar masculine energy.

Dominance can switch back and forth, but in my experience, I typically see *Ida* dominance in women and *Pingala* dominance in men. Because these flows feed the different sides of the brain, one also notices dominance in thinking patterns. The left brain is very linear and structural, good at mathematics and logical thinking. The right brain is more creative and abstract, thinking in broader, more conceptual, and intuitive terms.

Then there is the third channel that runs through the spinal region. It is called *Shushumna*, and it runs straight from the base of the spine through the crown of the head, up through all of the chakras.

Each chakra is located along the spinal region, with the seventh one residing above the crown. Most of these are located along with major nerve plexus such as the solar plexus and the cardiac plexus. Each chakra has a different frequency and basic characteristic, and, in the simplest ways, completely explains our journey through life.

Consider that you are a formless essence of consciousness. Consider that your true self has no body. It is completely expanded to infinity and part of a universal, unified field of consciousness, an eternal awareness. A choice is made for you to flow into a physical form, your beautiful avatar human body, to journey in the three-dimensional world on earth and create a human life experience.

You enter in through the root center, *Muladhara* Chakra. For men, this is located at the perineum, the space between the anus and the sex organs. For women, this is located at the cervix. As you enter the root chakra, you begin to experience yourself in physical form. You are a baby, completely vulnerable and beginning to experience the concept of mother, both your physical, care-giving mother and mother earth. Each are the providers of material support for you while in this body. As you begin your experience in the root center, you are working with the densest form of matter, earth itself.

This chakra rules your bones and all of the solid structures, like teeth, muscles, and tissues. It also rules the adrenal glands and large intestines. One learns to experience trust and vulnerability, and when that is challenged, fear is the emotion that results. In this center, the frequency matches the color spectrum of red, a slower-moving frequency closely related to the density of the element of earth.

When this center is out of balance, one may feel isolated and separate from everything else. Matters of basic survival become the challenge and focus of the life experience. The primary emotion of imbalance is fear because one perceives that the world is unsafe and that they are neither nurtured nor supported by the mother. This magnifies into belief patterns and behaviors of poverty consciousness, greed, survivalism, insecurity, and the inability to relate to one's own body or physical world.

Physical and psychological symptoms of imbalance may include obesity, hemorrhoids, constipation, arthritis, sciatica, and prostate issues, as well as self-indulgence, self-centeredness, insecurity, grief, or depression.

When balanced, one feels at home anywhere in the world. They trust in others and the universe to provide all material forms of life. They are financially grounded, physically healthy, fearless, alive, calm, and peaceful. The root chakra is also home to Kundalini *Shakti* energy.

As we rise up along the spinal journey, we come to the second chakra at the sacral center known as *Svadhisthana*. This is located on the tailbone, and the best way to find it is to close your eyes and gently squeeze the sphincter muscles within the anus, and notice where they tighten near the tailbone. This is the location of the second chakra. As you release the muscles, follow the release like an ocean wave as it flows toward the inside front body at the pubic bone. This is called the *Kshetram* or trigger point to access this chakra. When we apply pressure to the pubic bone, we trigger *svadhisthana*.

The color associated is orange, as its frequency matches this center and the element of water. In this center, we experience life through the lens of an individual and through our interactions with other individuals. These are intimate exchanges, including sexual relationships. We also begin to experience the world of duality: expanded and contracted, pain and pleasure, right and left hemispheres of the brain, hot and cold, and so on.

In addition, *Svadhisthana* is the center of creativity, where our pure source desires to both create and procreate. It is here in the very tissues of the body that we store our history of intimate and sexual relationships. The body parts associated are the womb, genitals, kidneys, and bladder. Governed by the water element, emotions are also associated with this center.

When out of balance, one may be afraid to risk intimate and loving relationships, and may fear the intensity of connection and attachment. On the flip side, one may confuse sexual energy for love and relax his or her boundaries in an attempt for deeper connection and nurturance. Mentally, this translates into desires that are unattainable. One may develop illusions and fantasies about relationship that are unrealistic. If one has suffered in intimate relationships, he or she may become judgmental, withdrawn, and angry. The natural flow of sexual energy may also take on the form of creativity or anger. If stifled or repressed, one can become anxious, reflecting the pent-up nature caused by resisting its natural and healthy flow.

Other symptoms of imbalance can include impotency; frigidity; uterine, bladder, or kidney trouble; lower back pain; frustration; anxiety; fears; being oversexed; and becoming self-centered.

When *Svadhisthana* is in balance, one is connected to the ability to give and receive. A natural flow of both giving and receiving becomes continuous as one integrates the knowing that they are both the same flow, moving in a complete cycle. One experiences self-love, self-esteem, self-acceptance, is emotionally self-sufficient, joyful, relaxed, and free both in feelings and in body. One is comfortable in the desire to express authentically.

The third chakra is called *Manipura*, which means the City of Jewels. This is located at the solar plexus and is home to 72,000 *nadis*, energy pathways, and can be found two-finger widths below the belly button, along the spine. The element of *Manipura* is fire and the color is yellow.

This is literally our center of transformation, governing the digestion of our physical food and metabolic processes, as well as the digestion of our life experiences. It is here that we begin to interact and experience groups, authority, and collective consciousness. From the fire of this center, we take action and begin to bring forward that which desires to be expressed and created into form and experience.

The body parts associated with this chakra are the digestive system, stomach, small intestine, pancreas, liver, spleen, and, again, the adrenals.

When out of balance, one may experience issues of powerlessness, greed, doubt, anger, shame, despair, and guilt. This can also include issues of self-abandonment, feeling empty and alone, and sometimes denial and escapism. At times, one experiences a lack of energy and vitality. One can be either overweight or underweight. The core belief underlying an imbalance is that one's existence depends on circumstances and people outside himself or herself. One sees obstacles everywhere and will conform and negate his or her own wishes and emotions to fit into the group.

This is a major gateway to measure integrity. Do we allow our true self to take action, or do we choke off the energy in trade for social approval?

Other symptoms of imbalance may include ulcers, diabetes, hypoglycemia, jaundice, hepatitis, and gallstones.

When balanced, one has integrity. One allows his or her truth to take form through action and show commitment, passion, and a flexibility to deal with change. One has good power, energy, digestion, and vitality.

The solar plexus chakra is our powerful point of projection. When we speak from this center, we propel our essence through the authentic expression.

Many people experience blocks here, and within all of the lower three centers. Society encourages mass conforming and a need for social approval versus individual expression. Society also encourages eating disorders and fear of authority through mass media campaigns to drive consumerism and system dependency. To be strong in this center, one needs a strong fire and strong core strength for the ability to be courageous to express one's power. Balance and strength result in healthy digestion of all of the experiences of life.

The fourth chakra is the heart center, *Anahata*, known as the home of the un-struck sound. Here, the element of air comes in with yet a higher frequency as we rise up the spine. It is met with the color of green.

The heart center has an electromagnetic field that is approximately fifty times larger than that of the brain's electromagnetic field. According to studies done at the HeartMath Institute, it is the heart that receives the incoming impulses first, as they approach the body.

As the frequency impulse comes into the field, the heart responds first and the brain follows. This suggests that the heart is the true brain of the avatar body system. Further, this allows the heart to serve as an immune system. As stimulus approaches, it may be determined if the frequency is harmonious to the body and it can be allowed into the field, or it can be deemed inharmonious and held out for further observation.

The heart center is located at the sternum or physical heart center. It is the center of unconditional love and compassion, where life's experiences are met with neutrality and observation, free of judgment and aversion. Body parts associated with the heart center are the cardiac plexus, heart, pericardium, lungs, thymus gland, and indirectly, the hands and arms.

When imbalanced, one can be emotionally shutdown, behave passively or insensitively. Sadness, depression, codependency, fear of abandonment, passive-aggressive nature, and over-attachment are symptoms of imbalance. One may lose himself or herself in the act of loving another, and when he or she does not receive love, he or she may become angry, compulsive and obsessive, and feel that love is conditional. Physical symptoms include asthma, high blood pressure, cardiovascular problems, arthritis, respiratory problems, stroke, and hypertension.

When balanced, one is compassionate, unattached and yet caring, devoted, free spirited, voluntarily simple in nature, open, calm, and in a state of gratitude. Energy pathways flow from the heart center down the arms and through the hands. When the heart center is activated and awakened, unconditional love and compassion are held in a container of pure, embodied faith and optimism.

The heart is also the balance point between the upper and lower triangles of chakras and serves to bridge the frequencies of heaven and earth.

Next is the throat chakra, *Vishuddhi*, known as the center of purification. It is here where the channel of our essence, in a distilled and focused form, is expressed through frequency into sound and, ultimately, into the word. This center is ruled by the element of ether. Ether is the void, the vacuum of space.

Through *Vishuddhi*, the power of the sound current is merged with the void to create the blueprints for our manifestations. This is a very powerful center within the system. It is here where the purity of our essence is then set into focused expression. We get to answer the question, "Am I the same person on the outside as I am on the inside?" This is where authenticity displays itself. This is the center that serves as the last filter of purification before our distilled intention is emitted through to form.

The chakra is located at the throat on the spine, centered between the Adam's apple and the V notch in the collarbone. The color frequency match is blue and body parts associated are the hypothalamus, thyroid, throat, ears, arms, hands, mouth, laryngeal plexus, and cervical spine. This is the gateway and bridge between the heart and the mind.

When imbalanced, obsession, pride, lack of expression, feeling repressed or creatively blocked, issues receiving and communicating one's truth, feelings and creativity arise. The belief that one is not being heard and understood can also arise. One feels physically stressed and unable to relax, and may carry the belief that his or her feelings or opinions are not valued. One may also rationalize what one says or does with a tendency toward desire, to impress, to knowingly deceive or manipulate. One may also appear to be disconnected from emotions as he or she strives to stay in mind.

Physical symptoms may include flu; neck ache; thyroid gland, parathyroid, and throat or vocal cord issues; and neck and shoulder issues.

When balanced, one expresses wisdom, has the ability to communicate fearlessly, honestly, clearly, confidently, courageously, and in a relaxed manner.

Yogi Bhajan said, "The highest, most effective energy on this planet is the word. There is nothing beyond it, and therefore, we must consciously understand the power of the word. If you honor the word, you will be honored in this world."

In the Bible, one can find the passage, "In the beginning, there was the word, and the word was God."

When the harmonized frequency of our entire spinal journey, all the way through to the throat center, is distilled into the sound expressed through the voice, a powerful process of manifestation is initiated. Through this expression, all elements merge into the void in a laser-like intention for creation. Like seeds planted in fertile soil, we soon reap what we sow. For that reason, it is essential to consciously choose our expressions, and clear up whatever is within us, so that it will match what we intend to create in our outer world. As above, so below, and as within, so without.

There is also a special relationship between the second and fifth chakras, the sacral and the throat. Not only do they share the same tissues, as in the example of the vagina and the throat tissues, but they also share a common function, creativity, and expression into form. While the lower center is more primal based and the upper is a more refined harmony of all of the centers merging, they both allow for the expression of the divine essence flowing through us.

The next chakra is *Ajna*, the third eye. It is located at the pineal gland, or pituitary in some traditions. These are both located near the center of the brain, between the temples. A psychic passageway leads out from the third eye center between the eyebrows and can be felt when the eyes are closed and turned upward and inward.

This is our center of perception, intuition, and literal inner vision. *Ajna* sits atop the spinal column at a place above duality, in a unified consciousness and merging point of the hemispheres of the brain.

It is here where we tap into universal consciousness and wisdom. It is here, in what is often called the command center of the body, where the true essence sits and governs once it ascends up the spine and through the chakra system. *Ajna* is the seat of the neutral mind.

Within our avatar body form is what I call the body-mind. It is not the essence of us but, instead, a highly sophisticated autopilot, computer-like system that is capable of reacting to all incoming stimulus. Through the recording of every sensory impression and resulting abstract rule for response, the subconscious mind acts as a storehouse or database of programming. The body-mind accesses this database at light speed to assess the proper reaction to all incoming stimulus. It sends the responses throughout the body via the nervous system.

Within the nervous system, various divisions look after everything from base operations of pumping the blood and breathing, to cycles of digestion and elimination, to appropriate reaction to danger in fight-and-flight response. The system is able to run without anyone sitting in the driver's seat. That's pretty cool.

Many people call this system, and the resulting personality, the ego. The ego gets a bad rap from many traditions and is often deemed as the enemy of the true essence, but I believe that the ego is like a child who simply needs proper guidance, and everyone knows what happens to children when the parents leave them to raise themselves. It's not usually pretty.

Within the autopilot mind, there are two major divisions: the negative and the positive mind. While we have touched on these earlier in the book, their importance is so profound that it warrants further discussion.

The negative mind's chief job is contraction. It is responsible for keeping your expanded form in the body and to ensuring that the body stays intact and safe. It looks at the incoming stimulus for risks to the health of the whole body system and it reacts with contraction of varying degrees, dependent on what is deemed appropriate by the programming. If the negative mind gets out of balance, it moves into fear, anxiety and, at its worst, paranoia.

The positive mind's chief job is expansion. Its job is to help your expanded, formless self express out into the three-dimensional world. It looks for opportunities to experience expansion. When it is out of balance, it will crave these experiences and move toward addiction.

As the negative mind over-contracts, it creates tension and can compact energy into densities, including eventual physical forms within the body itself. As the positive mind over expands, it can allow for holes in the electromagnetic field to appear. This allows for other energies to enter the body and experience your human form. Similar to going out of your house and leaving all of the doors and windows open, you never know what you will find when you return.

Each of these aspects runs directly off prior programming. The negative mind tends to be ruled by the past. A fire was hot and it burned us, so don't touch the fire. The positive mind tends to work on the dreams of the future and what wonderful things could be created. Each can pass to the other tense but neither really works in the present moment. It reacts in it.

This is where the neutral mind comes in. The neutral mind is the real you, the true divine essence of your fully expanded eternal self. As it enters the body, rises up the spine, and takes its seat at the top of the spinal column, above duality, it unifies the minds and takes time to respond to all of the information presented. This is where a conscious choice is made.

The conscious choice is made from a perspective of balance, neither over contracting nor over expanding, but simply allowing the experience to flow through. Whatever arises from the mind in that time is witnessed and released, allowing conscious editing of the programs, which will affect future autopilot reactions. In short, the process of conscious response becomes a lifelong practice of reprogramming the autopilot, and retraining the ego personality to serve the divine essence of the true aspect. With practice and clearing, the divine essence fully embodies and merges with the autopilot in true avatar form.

To recap, we enter the body through the base of the spine, and travel up through various elements and frequencies to experience duality and the illusion of being separate. As our consciousness rises, and we ascend in the body, we eventually come to sit at the third eye and take command of the ship.

In my own imaginings, I see the bridge of the Starship *Enterprise* from the popular TV and movie series of *Star Trek* within my head. At *Ajna*, there is a big leather chair. It is wide and comfortable with padded arms facing the panoramic view of my inner mind screen. On each side and slightly back from the captain's chair are two smaller swivel units. On one side sits the negative mind and on the other sits the positive mind.

When my true essence is fully embodied, it sits in the comfy chair, legs folded in easy pose as I comfortably command my own ship. My loyal autopilot aspects continuously feed me a flow of interpretation of the incoming stimulus, allowing me to make conscious choices and adjustments to their programming.

Whenever I feel the need to center myself, I sit and close my eyes, placing their inner focus at the third eye mind screen. This opens the energy circuit from the base of my spine all the way up to the third eye. Then I chant aloud or silently, "*Ong Namo Guru Dev Namo*," which translates to "I bow to the divine teacher within." This harmonic vibrates in my body and acts like the command of, "Beam me up, Scotty," and I come fully present in the seat of command.

From this space, we then express and bloom like a multi-petal lotus through the crown, remerging with the source from which we originate.

This crown is called *Sahasrara*, the thousand-petal lotus, but it is truly an infinite-petal lotus. The *Bihar* traditions believe that this is not actually a chakra because it is beyond the body. We work with it this way because it illustrates our full journey from oneness, through the valley of the shadow of death, a physical channel within our finite and temporary body vehicle. In this journey, we experience the illusion of separation and the experience of duality through the channels that split the current, only to remerge into oneness as we unify the duality and bloom in our own creations and connections to source and each other.

When you sit and consider all of this as possible, it is truly a profound and divine opportunity to learn to create in a rudimentary and mechanical way. And the creation machines are our bodies, being fueled and driven by our pure source essence. Life is truly a unique and miraculous gift.

To complete the model, let's revisit the play of energies that flow within this avatar form. The breath brings oxygen into the body to feed the cells through the blood, and expels the waste in the form of carbon dioxide and toxins that travel with it. The breath also brings in *Prana*.

*Prana* is a rejuvenative and healing life force energy. When it enters the body, it enters the cerebral spinal fluid and travels to the navel center. Within the navel center, where metabolic processes are driven, is another energy force known as *apana*. *Apana* is the eliminating force that moves downward to assist the elimination processes of the body. When *Prana* and *Apana* mix, they create the necessary ingredient to spark Kundalini energy to rise.

Kundalini energy, also known as Kundalini *Shakti*, resides at the base of the spine at *Muladhara* Root Chakra. Kundalini means the curl of the hair of the beloved and is often depicted as a coiled serpent ready to be awakened.

It's meaning can also be interpreted this way. *Kunda* is a word to describe a pit or cavity used for the sacred fires of initiation.

Kundalini energy is a powerful and activating force, and when awakened, it ascends the spine in three and one half spirals to pass through the chakras, activating them and awakening the corresponding centers of the brain.

If one imagines that the skull is in fact a *Kunda* or cavity and the brain a coiled and sleeping serpent, then one can see that the awakening of centers of the brain is a true initiation into states of higher consciousness or awareness. This is what raises our level of consciousness.

Yogi Bhajan clearly said that given forty days of practice, he could raise anyone's Kundalini. It was keeping it up that was the difficult part. Many of us have heard the stories of dramatic and debilitating Kundalini risings that were too intense for both body and mind. These are rare and usually the result of significant blockage in the channels and a mind not ready for integration of such change.

Most people are experiencing Kundalini energy in spurts that rise and fall, allowing for a more gentle timing of integration and overall ascension process. My own experiences have been a combination of these.

Within the thirty-day Kundalini teachers' training, I had daily runs of the energy up my spine in different degrees of temperature and sensation. Some days, the flow was light and bubbly; some days, sharp and forceful. Every day it ran. Every day it cleared.

On one occasion, it filled my inner vision with white light that appeared to extend all around my body in a large, expansive field. The sensation of travel up my spine was so wide and powerful that, for a moment, my mind wondered if I would shoot right out the top of my own head. As the thought crossed through my awareness, the little voice said, *"Well, you're in the right place if that should happen,"* and I just let go.

Once again, a flood of energy poured through me, leaving me in a state of bliss. The energy was neither hot nor cold, but electric. Once again, I felt like the goddess herself, free of the boundaries of mind, experiencing myself more deeply, embodied and expanded in the same moment.

The Kundalini training ended with me feeling like a Yoga teacher for the first time. I understood the flow of this energy on a deep, cellular level, and my capacity to hold the space for myself and others had reached a level of maturity and proficiency that was easily felt by all. I love to hold the space for deep transformation, and as with all awakenings, Kundalini is always present.

In my heart and soul, I knew that the times would come when people would flock to practices like these, perhaps not even knowing why. They would come because the raising of the Kundalini energy was inevitable by our sheer location in the solar system. The predictions of 2012 shift of ages spoke of frequency adjustments and their effect in raising consciousness. This could only happen with the aid of the energy itself.

People were going to need to have their nervous systems cleared and strengthened to hold the flow of energy. They were going to need lenses and frameworks within which to contain and process the experiences, ultimately raising their consciousness and level of self-awareness.

With the process of what I had done to that point, and the culmination of the month of intensive practice, I sat fully relaxed, strong, and aware in a way I had not before reached. What I once viewed as the intermittent magic of synchronicity was now my way of navigating life on a full-time basis. My little voice, as I call her, was fully in the body and comfortably choosing the next response. I began walking in full intuition, trusting my guidance implicitly. Life got way more interesting yet again.

# Chapter 12

The Kundalini training ended with an invitation to teach at the center. This was exactly what I needed to launch into sharing all that I have been given. I was very grateful to Sraddha for extending the opportunity.

I stayed in Sedona and began to experience a deeper level of guidance that follows as you listen and open your channel. It seems that the wider you allow the flow to enter the body, the wider the opportunities.

I woke one morning to the sound of the little voice saying, *"You should distribute these pendants."* By "these pendants," the little voice was referring to the Quantum Vibrational Stones that carry harmonic codes. They are treated in a technology known as quantum generators, a technology developed by David Sereda.

David is a brilliant man in a lifelong practice of meditation and scientific exploration. In addition to these endeavors, he is also a filmmaker.

I had purchased a plain hematite stone a year prior at a local Sedona jewelry store and noticed that it made me more stable in my energy. I would ensure to wear it when I worked on the computer, talked on a cell phone, or flew on an airplane. It kept my energy more even and clear. Although I knew little about why that worked, its effect was obvious to me.

I rose from my sleep and ventured out into my day to purchase a *djembe* drum for my son. A local musician named Three Trees, a very talented and beautiful soul, was selling the drums and I headed for his house. Upon arrival, a mutual friend, John Dumas, was leaving as I was arriving, and in a split second, John pointed out that we were wearing the same pendant.

I laughed and shared my little voice's prompting and he pulled his cell phone from his pocket. "Let me connect you," he said. "David Sereda is a good friend of mine."

Within a few short hours, I had a vision, was in contact with David, and was his newest distributor.

The Quantum Vibrational Stones, to me, are like highly tuned, energetic tea bags that we steep in our energy field. David writes harmonic codes into the atomic structure of the stones and wire through his technology. This can be viewed as similar to writing a movie into a disk. Once the harmonic code is in the stone, it stays written in.

As the stones interact with the field of an individual, their body voltage increases. This had been demonstrated and measured with a simple electrician's multi-meter, measuring in millivolts. A base reading would be taken by placing the electrode tips between the thumb and first finger of the subject's hands. Then a stone would be placed between the fingers and the subject would be measured again. The increase in body voltage varied subject to subject and design to design.

A GDV Aura Camera system was also used to study the effects of the treated stones on an individual's field. Images were captured without the stone and with the stone. Results showed an overall increase in the body voltage, a brightening of the aura field, and an alignment and increased energy in the chakra system.

The base harmonic that David uses is NASA's recording of the Sound of the Sun. This is a harmonic that represents pure life force energy. Additional harmonics could be added such as prayers and mantras.

I quickly began to experiment by adding in mantra. The first run contained two mantras. The first is OM, the universal sound of expansion and creation. The second one is the *Adi* Mantra, *Ong Namo Guru Dev Namo*. *Ong Namo Guru Dev Namo* is my base mantra. It is chanted three times at the beginning of every 3HO Kundalini Yoga class and quickly helps me open my channel and tune myself in. The mantra translates to, "I bow to the divine teacher within," and, when chanted, connects one to his or her true divine self and all of the infinite wisdom of all teachers that come before them in their lineage.

When I wore the pendant treated with these, I felt both an anchoring of myself within the body, but also the essence of what I wanted to express expanding beyond me. It is a powerful recipe.

Mantras have become a large part of my life, as when one is played in a space, it quickly clears the energy. When chanted in my body, it attunes my energy and cells to a set frequency that is healing. Different mantras have different effects, and so a person can pick and choose one to suit a present need.

What I love about the pendants is that they seem to choose their owners. I can walk through a crowded airport and have a person walk boldly over to me to ask what I'm wearing and how he or she can get one. This happens a lot! I love to be the carrier of such a profound technology working with a living stone being and sharing them with those they're called to. People from all over the world seek these stones and report back various changes in their lives. For me, they have brought me a consistent energy flow and, together with all of the modalities and practices I engage in, I feel that they assist in amplifying my prayers.

# Chapter 13

The inner guidance was now beginning to give me direct instruction on what to do in every moment, and the next thing it said was, *"White Tantra."*

Twice a year, the 3HO organization creates a gathering on the solstice to align with this powerful time of year, while immersing in community and practice. Special classes are held along with an International Peace Prayer Day and three days of White Tantra.

The summer event is held in Espanola, New Mexico, and the winter event is in Lake Wales, Florida. This particular year, I went to both. Summer was first.

I drove from Sedona to Espanola and ventured up the hill to the sacred site gathering. Most attendees camped in tents and trailers, but some of us stayed in basic cabins. The event lasted for about a week and was filled with multiple options for experiencing teachers and classes.

Each participant received a camp work assignment as we collectively housed, fed, and cleaned up after one another. It was a beautiful collection of souls and I felt so welcome the moment I arrived.

The first few days were filled with Aquarian *Sadhana* practices starting at 3:15 a.m. Hundreds of us, dressed all in white, would gather for a *kriya* and chanting. It was so powerful to practice and chant with that many souls. The energy of the camp was amping up every hour. In addition to morning practices, the days were filled with various topics and classes. I kept myself busy and enjoyed all of the new friends I was making.

Toward the end of the week was the three days of White Tantra. It was what all of the participants were talking about and waiting for. My Kundalini teacher, Hari Jap, had shared some of his experiences, but I knew I would not really know what it was until I had my own.

According to the traditions and the teachings of Yogi Bhajan, there is a *Mahan* Tantric, a person who incarnates on the planet to serve as one who can ground the negative energy of thought and emotion, sending that energy into the earth for transmutation. When Yogi Bhajan was alive, he served in that role. Upon his death, his subtle body continued to serve in this capacity, being focused or moderated by an appointed person. There are a few of these people who serve to hold the space for these practices, who travel the planet and lead daylong meditations in various cities. At the solstices, they concentrate the practices and have three full days instead of one.

Day one arrived and we all excitedly flooded to secure our spots. Within an open-sided, airplane-hangar-like building, approximately 900 of us sat knee to knee in long lines. Typically, this formation was males on one side and females on the other, except where sheer matching did not work.

Participants would gather each of the days to sit in thirty-one- and sixty-two-minute meditations. Some of the meditations would involve strange postures and mudras (finger positions), and typically, the eyes would be fixed in a gaze with the partner in front of you while you chanted a mantra. Sometimes, we would chant, and sometimes, we would whistle. They were all quite peculiar and yet fun at the same time.

I was very lucky in my first experience as a wonderful acupuncturist from the US agreed to be my partner for the first day. He was very experienced and completely able to hold all of the positions for the full times. His strength was powerful and gave me the ability to match him in my commitment to the postures. They were intense. Legs may start to fall asleep, arms and muscles may shake, and the tension and compression within the body may activate deep, cellular clearing of stuck energies and thought forms.

The energy, which is said to flow up and down the lines in a zigzag format, cut through the subconscious blocks as it passed through the participants.

When day two came, my new friend and I chose to be partners again; we were absolutely delighted by the results we had on day one. By the third day, we were energetically glued and having profound clearings supported by the other polarity. He is a beautiful soul and a lovely friend.

For the first set of the morning on the third day, we just sat and prepared ourselves mentally. The air was very scintillating. I sat with spine straight and eyes closed, and began to feel an energy current travel up the path of the line directly to me. It felt as though it was coming from the right side of the line. In my mind's eye, I could see the face of a man so distinct and clearly. This was very interesting to me, and so I stayed within the mind, gazing into his smiling and beautiful face. He was radiant.

The set was beginning so I positioned myself, smiled at my wonderful partner, and we began. I believe I had my left arm raised parallel to the floor, with elbow bent and peace fingers resting above my eyebrow. It was as though I was saluting my partner. My right arm was bent at the elbow and tight to the body with thumb and first finger joined in *gyan* mudra at the level of my shoulder. We held the position for sixty-two minutes and chanted the whole time.

It didn't take long for the sensation to build in my body. It began in the heel of my left foot and, like a circuit, moved up to the knee, then to the hip, and then transferred through the pelvis to the right hip. From there, it continued to the right knee and heel, and the circuit continued to flow. The sensation was intense but still moving at a pace I could follow with my awareness around and around through my legs and my hips. Then it sped up to a point where it was just this constant sensation throughout the entirety of the circuit. My lower body was vibrating with intense sensation that was rapidly becoming painful.

Because of all my prior training, I was used to intense Yoga practices that would raise sensation and activate clearings. The practice filled me with excitement as I wondered what was actually happening within this circuit of meridians within my body. It was fascinating to me so I simply watched it.

Soon, the sensation began to rise up my spine and cause my body to shake. When you think of the stress reaction of an animal, like a deer for example, you can see the pattern they take and how important the shaking is at the end of a stress response. For example, a deer senses a predator and the mind sends it into a fight-or-flight response. The deer begins to run. The hormones within the body serve to open the blood vessels and allow the heart to pump more fuel to the limbs for action, which, in this case, is running. A lot of contraction happens as the muscles are fired and impact occurs with earth as each hoof touches the ground.

Once the deer feels she is out of danger, she stops and she shakes. She fully shakes the body right from the core and out through all of the extremities. It is profound and simple, and she hangs onto nothing of the contractions that she experienced moments earlier.

When energy begins to pour through circuits in the body and actually invites the body to shake, this is a form of significant release. As the shaking began in my body, I fully surrendered and then it increased. As it increased, the intensity of the sensation was now fully fuelling the circuit within my legs and up the full length of my spine. Partners on either side of us began to lose their gaze as my peripheral vision caught glimpses of their eyes moving toward me. I stayed fixed on my partner's eyes as he held a beautiful space of strength for me. It was so incredible.

Once I felt that the pain could not possibly be more intense, a sudden and distinct change occurred. The wave of sensation that had been so painful crossed through the center of its own polarity and became ecstatic pleasure. Yes! Can you imagine?

I was a woman sitting across from a man, first vibrating in intense, painful sensations, then suddenly, in full-blown orgasmic release throughout every pathway in her body. It felt like it lasted ten minutes, but I honestly have no concept of the time in reality.

It was such a profound experience of realizing how the mind held the determination of pain or pleasure. I had not changed anything in what I was doing. I did not move, I did not stop breathing or chanting, nor did I stop gazing into my partner's eyes. The only thing that changed was my mind's perception of the sensation. Somehow, as I simply witnessed and allowed it to be, the channels cleared and the sensation flipped from pain to pleasure. It literally felt like it passed through a portal from one polarity to the other.

I could have contracted into the experience, tightening as the sensations escalated. I could have let it escalate in that contraction, forcing me to stop or move, but instead, I remembered that the mind contracts the body and that everything is about perception and focus.

I kept hearing the gentle voice of my true self coach me by inviting the positive mind to see the potential release and expansion. At the same time, I imagined the rewards that would come by holding a neutral mind space of awareness. I held the posture knowing that "this, too, shall pass" and always knowing that I had the choice to move. For my efforts, the universe gave me the gift of experiencing the opposite polarity, as the sensation broke from one side of the coin and straight through to the opposite side in pure, ecstatic pleasure.

Once the set had ended and I was ready to enter into the world, I began to look around the room. Three sets of yogis to my right was the man in the vision at the beginning of the practice. I was very curious.

At the end of the third day of Tantra they do a special practice called the blind walk. In this practice, one person serves as leader and a string of others connect and follow them. Each holds hands with the person in front and behind, while alternating the way each one faces to maintain a balanced and straight line.

I gathered in a line with about ten others, and our leader led us around as we all closed our eyes and trusted her to guide us. The idea was to teach us absolute trust of putting one foot in front of the other without knowing where we were going. Our leader, bless her soul, was not really skilled at ensuring that we didn't get hurt, so a lot of people experienced the effects of bumping into rocks and stumps. It didn't take long before a bunch of them bailed out and our line began to cinch up.

Guess whose hand took my left palm firmly in his. The man three yogi sets to the right, the one in my vision earlier in the morning. As soon as our palms joined, an energy circuit formed between them like a vortex of energy perfectly matched and now in sync. Even as I write, I can feel this. This continued as we felt such a depth of connection to one another in a beautifully merged exploratory syncing that woke every cell in my body. Were we somehow energetically connected souls, perfectly suited to run these circuits that now joined into each other's bodies. I could feel the warmth of his heart as though my body had extended and joined with his. I was mesmerized as our leader continued to guide us blindly around.

Did our mere presence in the same Tantra line ignite this wondrous experience? I had never felt such a palpable connection before in my life and my whole being was excited. We kept our eyes closed and simply vibrated as one body. When the line game stopped, this man promptly pulled me aside in awe of the experience and we embraced. We introduced ourselves and I ran away as quick as I could politely do so.

It had not been long enough since I had separated from my partner and I was so afraid of any connection. This was something completely unknown, both exciting me and scaring me in a way that I could not deal with. I have thought about this man so many times since that day and what a gift of possibility he gave me.

Here I had come, in search of self-realization. I wanted to feel comfortable in my own body. I wanted to feel relaxed, safe, and confident in my interaction with the world. Now I was not only in my body, I was connected with my true self. I was conscious that my mind was not me. I was experiencing the flow of energy and the universe through my body. I was expanding from an anchored point within my very core. And now the universe was showing me how much more incredible connection with another human could be. This was so far off the charts of anything I had experienced with another person before. I was once again in awe.

The pathways in my body were fully surrendered to source energy and the essence of who I am. Now, that energy was seeking to merge outside with others. Yes, I could sense the subtleties of earth energy, different with each mass and form. I could feel the magic of sacred sites, crystals, and frequency-infused objects of prayer and programming. I could read the emotions and energies of people, but I had never connected so fully and energetically with anyone like that before. It was as if the matter that made up our bodies was irrelevant. Our energy current merged like two separate streams meeting at a fork in the river.

I lay awake all that night in my bunk, fantasizing about finding that mysterious and beautiful man in a camp of

1,800 beings. I lay awake wondering what a more physical connection would feel like. It all felt too soon. I was as scared as I was mesmerized. This proved to be my new way of life. Everything that followed carried both polarities of experience at once. My path, the neutral mind zero point, would ask me to balance it all.

I drove away the next morning. I liked the idea that this experience could be preserved as magic. Maybe one day, I would be ready to know him, or maybe one day, it would happen again with another. I was certain that I would seek it out and the universe would bring it when I was ready. The bar on connection had been raised to an entirely new level; nothing less would ever do again.

# Chapter 14

The next instruction my little voice gave was "*Vipassana.*" *Vipassana* is a form of meditation. It was brought to North America through the teachings of a man in India named Goenka. It is based on the teachings of the Buddha.

Sits, as they are called, are done in groups for extended periods. One begins with a ten-day sit. I arrived in Calgary that August following one more short trip to Sedona for a class called Conflict Resolution.

The Conflict Resolution was the last piece I needed to complete my 500-hour Yoga teacher's certification. The class was four days and, through the lens of the Yoga sutras, a basic philosophy of understanding, we examined the origin of conflict within us. Sraddhasagar led the class in her usual framework of structure, fully guided by what was happening in the moment. She is amazing at this.

Within the class, we came to realize, through experiential learning, that all conflict arose from within and was the result of an unfulfilled need. While it was easy to know this in theory, Sraddha's method allowed us to embody the knowledge and embed a habit of looking within to resolve our issues. It is a profound practice of looking at what manifests around you as a direct mirror. We call in the reflections and experiences we need to give us a deeper look at ourselves. Conflict Resolution, as taught by Sraddhasagar, based on the teachings of Rama Joyti Vernon, is a highly effective method of understanding this truth.

Arriving in Calgary, I gave myself three days to relax and chill out in a hotel. Soon, I would arrive at the door of the *Vipassana* retreat and spend ten days in silence, learning and practicing this meditation technique. I really enjoyed myself on the days that led up to it.

I watched movies, had massages, ate decadent meals, and generally just rested. On the way to the retreat, I stopped to catch Nicolas Cage's newest release of the *Sorcerer's Apprentice*. I realized as I sat in the theatre that I had not been in a theatre for quite a long time. The music began and every cell in my body vibrated, so fully open and easily effected by the frequency. It was so exciting as waves of sensations raced across the surface of my skin! I was truly alive in a whole new way.

After the movie, I drove out to the residence in Conrich, a subdivision just outside Calgary. A lovely family that deeply believed in the meditation practice had built their house specially to accommodate the retreats a couple of times a year. When those times arrived, the furniture would get moved to the garage and the whole 6,000-square-foot residence would turn into a dorm room meditation center. It was very nice!

We arrived, signed in, and turned over our keys and wallets for safekeeping. We weren't being held prisoners, but leaving would mean asking for our items, and while we meditated, we could be relaxed knowing that they were secured.

First time attendees were completely looked after. Meals were made for us and the dorms were kept clean for us. Return students came in as volunteers, part time serving and part time meditating.

The first three days, we learned to simply focus our awareness on the breath coming in and out of the nostrils. All the while we kept silent, not even nodding or acknowledging one another. I had never experienced this silence before and was surprised at how relaxing and comfortable it was to just let go of all of the social niceties and need to communicate. We were allowed to fully immerse in ourselves. That was decadent!

By day two, a character popped into my awareness field and began to talk to me. This was all in my mind, but the conversation was very interesting. It was a witty banter back and forth and would have made an excellent screenplay. It was filled with intrigue and romance as the man began to attempt to connect with me energetically.

Every now and then, I would remember that I was supposed to be meditating and I would try to block the image, but the man would keep talking to me. My mind began to wonder if it were really happening on some other level of existence and that the whole thing was real. Then I would flip to the logic that my very bored mind was inventing fantasies to avoid being quieted down.

Day three arrived. We would meditate for segments of one to two hours, and this would go on all day and into early evening, except for meal times. Following the breath in and out of the nostrils was making me wonder if I might go insane. But I kept up. We lost one woman, whose last words were, "I'm sure if I stay another minute, I'll go crazy."

The mind is a powerful critter. My Meditation Man showed up again. The conversation was awesome. He flirted with me and I was drawn down a road of fun and fantasy, and then I realized once again that I was supposed to be meditating. I made a deal with him. I agreed to meet him, in person, after the retreat. I was going to be in Banff, so I suggested a time and location. This way, I could be left alone, and if he were real, I dared him to prove it. He agreed and was gone. He was really gone, and of course I missed him.

Day four brought the actual *Vipassana* technique into our practice. We were to begin by scanning the surface of our skin for sensation. We started at the top of the head and worked our way slowly to the bottom of our feet. As the sensation was noticed, we would just watch it, no judgment and no aversion. No craving for the pleasant, bubbly sensations and no aversion to the burning or piercing ones. We just watched.

As we watched and witnessed, the sensations would change. Dense ones would release and the bubbly ones would expand. It all felt good and it all felt intense, and I was very engaged in the process. Sometimes, the dissipation of a density would bring feelings or thoughts; occasionally, it was memories. Always, it was release. I felt like an energetic doctor surgically clearing the whole surface of my body.

Next, we began to sweep the body from top to bottom but also bottom to top. As soon as we began this, my mind instantly converted the experience to that of my body being a hologram. Instead of sticking to the surface of my body, I was deep within it. This was exactly the same as the medical intuitive training I had taken with Wanda in Sedona. I could sink my awareness into every cell and inch of my innards.

The process became so fascinating and I would cycle up and down, and up and down. I found myself meditating through the entire night. The process left me in a constant state of relaxation, and even sleep did not matter one bit. In one of the meditation segments, I dropped deeply into my spine and found what felt like the epicenter of the most base postural contraction of fear. I felt like Indiana Jones on hunt for sacred treasure. And I had found it!

I allowed myself to just witness the point. It burned like a hot needle in my neck. I just held my awareness with it. Soon, the sensation began to expand and the density of it became lighter as the temperature cooled to a warm, steady glow. My awareness stayed with it as it drew my attention through passages of muscles, out into my left arm and up into my head.

Then I realized that it was taking the path of my car accident in the tissues of my body. Everywhere I had been hurt was now being deeply released.

Day ten arrived and, at mid-morning, the silence broke. *"Five more days!"* was my inner voice's chant as I was still so immersed in the process. It was over and it was time to reintegrate into the community of fellow meditators.

The sounds of the voices were overwhelming, so I sought the refuge of the backyard to slow the transition. I was not alone. I marveled at the lesson of how we view people. When you sit in silence for ten days with strangers, your mind begins to create ideas of who they are and what they will sound like.

Most of those were pretty close, but some were completely off the mark. I laughed as I realized this and promised myself to always open my heart and eyes to receive whatever one would share with me, rather than let my mind create a false perception.

This entire practice was provided by donation only. Each participant was being supported by one who had donated at an earlier event, and now was our opportunity to offer what we could. What a beautiful concept.

The *Vipassana* technique of meditation goes right into the tissues of our vessel to directly address contracted experiences, thoughts, and emotions. As we hold a neutral space of observation, the contraction and its source are invited to simply leave the body. This opens the body and it releases the patterns and beliefs that are loaded within the contraction. It frees the mind of the impulse that fuels future reactions. This is deep and profound healing in the most useable and simple form.

Combined with the Yoga practices, one can change his or her whole experience in life. I am certain that this technique would allow one to completely heal the body, mind, and soul. I look forward to my next sit. Ten days of being in silence alone is worth it.

# Chapter 15

The immersion in all of the practices experienced this year was heightening my sense of self. Not only did I perceive in most moments from the perspective of my true self, but I was palpably aware of all of the energies within my body and all around it. Everything began to be experienced through energetic merging.

My mind became witness for its thoughts, but the world was being experienced through my skin and the vibrations within and around my body. My dear friend, Barb, quickly labeled me an energy junky, as I sought to satisfy the urge to feel everything through this new sensory experience.

Now off to Peru!

Peru was about reunion. Not only did I once again gather with a beautiful soul family, but the sacred lands of this country were reawakening my energetic senses in a way that the mind could only sit and witness. The physical sensations of every stone and every pathway merged with my body and tickled my cells.

Just like in France, every second night, I would lay awake, feeling the sensation of energy streaming into my crown, as though being downloaded with data and coding. The sensation would leave me quiet and attentive, free of thought and relaxed in my emotions. Even though sleep would be considerably limited, I felt awake and present in every breath.

Peru has an even more special quality that emanates from the people. Their hearts are open and they shine through their eyes. When you meet, a connection is welcomed in the gaze and you feel free of resistance to their purity of intent. Yes, there are the touristy areas where one feels like a walking dollar bill at times, but this is such a small percentage of the experience that it seems insignificant.

I arrived late in the evening to Lima and was met by our group leaders, Aluna Joy and Raphael. They are well known for their connections to Star Elders and the Angelic Realms, and offer many sacred site journeys around the globe. I had tried to get into their trip the year before but was met with a waiting list. Their journeys fill fast, so one must follow the impulse and trust that spirit is aligning you for the perfect timing.

The thing I loved most about the trip with these beautiful souls was all of the free time they planned into the schedule. I always felt relaxed and in the perfect flow. That is a challenge within a group of thirty people or more.

Aluna and Raphael whisked us away to an overnight hotel and I was happy to greet the pillow with my head. The next morning, we rose and had breakfast in the lobby. Throughout the night, the remaining early-bird journeyers had arrived. We would head to Cuzco to acclimatize to the altitude and rest for a couple of days before the remaining group joined us.

Once again, we were shuttled to the airport, and as we stood, waiting to move through the system, four women surrounded me. Like me, they could sense energy and most of them could also see the energy. They had spotted the pendant around my neck and were fascinated by its dance of energy and its amplification of my aura.

I was wearing a Brazilian Blue Quartz Quantum Vibrational Pendant in a Sunray design. It is beautiful and this particular stone was treated with NASA's recording of the sound of the sun and the mantras *OM* and *Ong Namo Guru Dev Namo*. Together, they created a potent harmonic of life-giving force with an invitation for my true self to be in body and then expanded in all directions. These individuals had opened up the ability to sense and see it. It was fun for me to hear their points of view.

That was when Ryan walked over to me and smiled. Ryan is 6'4" tall and I had to bend my neck back quite a ways to meet his gaze. He had been fully opened by a sudden Kundalini awakening while attending a workshop many months earlier. The rush of the energy moved through him with such intensity that it blew open all of the veils, leaving Ryan able to see all energy and sense the truth in every aspect. His eyes shone like that of a saint and everyone simply loved to be near his field for the blissful and gentle shower of unconditional love that emanated from him. We would become great friends.

When I look back on the trip, it's hard to describe the amount of gifts I received. Peru was an invitation and practice to connect beyond the boundaries of my own form. It had many lessons for me.

Our journey began in Cuzco, getting used to the elevation. Some of our group struggled, as their bodies needed time to adjust blood consistency and oxygen levels. I woke with a mild headache the first morning and headed straight for a latte shop. I hadn't been drinking any coffee for some time, but the little voice in my head assured me that it would open my blood vessels and allow everything to ease. Whether that makes sense scientifically or not didn't matter. Within ten minutes of beginning to drink the warm and soothing drink, my headache was gone. Between lattes and coca tea, I was fine the entire time.

Each site we would visit would greet me with a palpable connection. I could almost see the energy moving in the space, and on some occasions, I did. There was a blue hue over everything. At first, I didn't notice it, but then Ryan prompted me to remove my sunglasses, and after that, I saw it all the time.

Every site opened my heart a little more and expanded my field a little greater. All of my essence was reaching out to touch the earth I was standing upon. Every stone and pathway had its own signature of frequency. Some felt good and some felt foreign. I loved that I could talk with the group and we could share our observations in a language that was helping me to deepen my understanding of the experience.

When we arrived in the sacred valley, we landed at a sweet little hotel along the river. A large grass area was perfect for morning Yoga and evening stargazing. What was supposed to be a short visit became extended when a national transportation strike occurred. This was good because some of the group had contracted the tourist bug and were sticking close to bathroom and bed.

Ryan was one who was afflicted, and one of the women in the group suggested that he back breath with another to help clear his channel. The woman saw that it should be me. At dinner, Ryan asked if I would help, and

I was grateful for the invitation. Ryan's energy is so beautiful and there was a deeper connection between us that created curiosity and a little fear.

Ryan was married, and although he was traveling alone, one needed to not confuse the excitement of connection with the urge for sexual interaction. At this point, my body didn't know how to differentiate. The attraction would prove challenging, and yet the boundaries were crystal clear. In that regard, it was the perfect experience of connection because the lines were drawn in advance.

After dinner, I went up to his room and he instructed me in the practice. We were to sit back to back and begin to breathe in the same pattern. I turned around and began my descent toward the edge of the bed when my spine lit up as energy shot to the top of my head like a carnival game of hammering the base to ring the bell.

I let out an audible "whoa!" sound only to hear it being echoed with Ryan doing the same. Our spines both lit up and merged before our bottoms hit the surface of the bed. I was mesmerized by the sensation joining us energetically as we sat back to back. We both breathed up and down our own spines at the same pace and then imagined the spinal columns merging. My grounded and healthy state intended to help fuel and clear his field so that he would begin to feel better.

The lines between our spines had disappeared and our energetic bodies were merging. This was becoming confusing, as my heart began to expand and merge in a loving and deep connection. This man was married and all of my boundaries were gone. Without thought or censoring, my lips communicated that he would have to be the one to stop this because I had no boundaries left.

We sat a moment longer, back to back, in one big field of vibration, much like the experience at summer solstice with the man in the blind walk. Our fields somehow connected and merged in a way that was so seamless and easy. Was it because we were a special connection or that we were simply open to connection? I couldn't answer that, but I knew that this was the only kind of connection I would want with a man.

We stopped a few minutes later. Without the ability for words, I quickly said good night and returned to the grassy, open area to lie on my Yoga mat and gaze at the stars. What had just happened and how would I think of anything else?

The energy is so wise as it worked to vibrate up all of the possible thoughts and emotions that surround the subject of connection with a man. The boundaries were laid out and my whole body wanted to make them disappear. Did that make me a bad person? I knew that I would have acted on the impulse if given the opportunity. This was very confusing. There was another person involved and what on earth was I thinking?

The next day became a free day as we waited to be able to move once again on our journey, so I sought the refuge of a Star Elder Reading with Aluna. Within the reading, she told me that it was time for me to get naked. She pointed out that I was so careful in how I shared myself, my views, and connections with the world. She said that it was time for me to really let myself be seen. She kept repeating, "It's time to get naked, Angela."

I knew what she meant. In all my years of fitting in, I would rarely let myself be truly seen, as it was much easier to match myself to the surroundings, like a chameleon, than to show my true colors and risk being excluded.

After lunch, a few of us decided to go on a cross-country adventure by foot. We had spotted a waterfall off in the distance, and with a little guidance from some local boys, we were on our way.

I walked out ahead of the group, deep in my own contemplation. I kept hearing the sound of Aluna's voice as she repeated the mantra, "It's time for you to get naked, Angela." Soon, her voice faded and my own little voice was at it. Today was the perfect day for a ceremony—the perfect ceremony for me to truly allow myself to be naked in the world. Today would be about absolute authenticity, here in the sacred lands of Peru on a magical walk in the valley.

The nearer we came to the waterfall, the hotter my body became. The humidity mixed with the exertion of the walk was making me perspire and I could suddenly feel the freshness of the water as its rushing sounds bounced against my skin. We were getting nearer. Then my true self showed me the picture of what was to come. I was going to get in that water. I was going to strip all of my clothes off and get naked in Peru in the rush of cold, flowing natural water. This was going to be my ceremony. I walked faster.

Somehow, when the little voice decides to approach a proverbial cliff of discomfort, it stabilizes my mind into quiet surrender. There was no argument in the back of my head. No pros and cons list, no rush of fear bubbling to the surface, and there was no contraction in my body. I walked with even more intent.

Soon, it became obvious that we would not reach the foot of the waterfall itself but would meet up with the rushing stream that flowed from it and emerged from the thick woods. As the end of our trail appeared in my view, my arms immediately crossed as my hands grasped the bottoms of my white shirt and began to raise it over my head. I was still walking.

My shirt landed in the branches of the tree, quickly followed by my bra and remaining clothes, sandals flung softly ahead of me. I never really stopped, but instead stepped into the rush of water, completely naked, and made my way deeper up the stream. From behind me, I heard the lovely voice of my dear friend, Helena, as she said, "Oh shit, now I have to do it, too!" This was her light and funny way of excitedly saying, "Woo-hoo!" Helena was tons of fun and joyfully quick in her wit.

I turned around and immersed my body under the cascade of flowing water as it rushed over the rocks above me. Fully exposed to the air and the group behind me, my breath was taken as the droplets hit my body and rinsed all impurity from my field. I was being reborn. I was being cleared and awakened in all of my senses, as I lay fully exposed and completely naked in that stream. In my mind, I uttered the words; "*I am completely naked now and forevermore.*"

A sense of relaxation was felt more deeply than ever before. Three other souls joined in my ritual and we all felt a sense of such freedom for the experience. It was a good day.

Later in the evening, I once again returned to the lawn to lie on my Yoga mat and take in this brilliant sky. I could hear the sound of the river just feet away as it rushed along. Soon, the lawn was covered with other members of the group and a bonfire off in the distance was lit.

Ryan arrived and sat with me on my mat. Each of us was so curious about the sensations of the energetic merge we had experienced that we had to do it again. Sitting back to back, the experience resumed instantly with a smooth coupling of our energy bodies, merging the vortexes of their flow. Once again, there were no boundaries and no words. This time our hands found the others and our fingers gently interlaced.

Our dear friend, Mark, joined us, and the three of us then lay on our backs, gazing up at stars and telling each other stories of our lives to deepen our connection. Mark is the most beautiful and magical being gracing our planet with his presence. He is absolutely otherworldly. He was in such delight to be in the company of others who could understand the world in the way he sees it. A talented acrobat with a worldwide career in circus, Mark was first and foremost a beautiful, genuine, and real heart-driven person.

The three of us lay there under the stars, I was in the middle, and all of us covered in a layering of alpaca ponchos and blankets. It was cozy family, three peas in a pod. We were a reunited family of souls, and although I didn't consciously know the details of our connections, it was plain as the nose on my face that we had all journeyed together before.

As our hands all joined, the vortex in my left hand, the one in Ryan's care, opened and coupled with his like two machines docking perfectly into one another. In a split second, our arms were one and the merging of the energy continued through our bodies. We just lay in the space with Mark and allowed all of our cells to vibrate. The three of us were the pure harmonic of bliss and love.

Hours passed by with little to say, only blissful sensations and relaxation, as we gazed up at a brilliant sky filled with stars. Our entire fields were being cleared, upgraded, and merged. I didn't want it to stop. Mark rose, looked at us both in awe, and just said, "Wow!" as he walked off to bed.

Within a few moments, I found my head upon Ryan's chest in a much deeper embrace. It felt so good. My boundaries were nonexistent and I knew that nothing would stop me from continuing into a deeper merging. But in my heart, I knew that would be a recipe for regret. We were not the only ones to consider, and despite the fact that this was a rare and beautiful connection of energy, it didn't align with deeper core values.

I rose, smiled, and muttered something about a cold shower. Then I went off to my room. The next day, we were both relieved that I had done this and we also knew that we couldn't connect this way again.

While that was a challenge for the mind that craves sensation and a heart that longs for this kind of connection, the essence part of us was just grateful to be in each other's field again. I didn't know our connection, but I knew we had one that spanned lifetimes.

It was as though our systems were just an energetic match. I was completely grounded by his flow as it merged with mine and sent me into the earth. When we connected, I felt whole, which gave me a perspective of what that truly felt like. This would be one of the many gifts.

I remember my dear roommate, Julie, a very wise woman from Canada. Julie's energy was so soft, centered, and loving, and she really honored her inner guidance to be quiet and observe on the trip. She took so much in and created magical experiences for herself as she followed this guidance. She could see the dynamics between Ryan and me, and expressed concern for my heart.

I remember turning to her as I was placing clothes in my suitcase, a smile radiating across my face. I simply said, "I would endure whatever my heart must go through to know three weeks of being in this field, than to have endured a lifetime of never knowing it." There was no illusion of the reality of our friendship. In logical terms, none of it made sense anyway. This was a deep and energetic connection between us, and a gift of opening and calibration. I knew that we came together to open channels and gain a palpable, embodied knowledge of what wholeness feels like. This mission had already been accomplished.

The first day, when Ryan reached out his hand to shake mine as we stood in the Lima airport, the sleeve upon his arm slid up. On his wrist, and in fact on both wrists, was a tattoo. The tattoo was simply the shape of a downward pointed triangle inside a circle. Ryan had the same symbol on each wrist as I had seen on the little etheric plate that Wanda pulled from my third eye two years prior. The same symbol that echoed in my head as the words *"sun alignment"* and *"shift is coming"* passed through me. The same symbol that caused both Wanda and my little voice to say, *"This has to do with Peru. Write that down."*

The fun of Peru was just beginning as heightened awareness in the cells of my body was now leaping around in blissful connection to everything. And I mean everything! People, stones, air currents, trees, animals, and the ground itself. I felt through my feet, my breath, my eyes, and my skin. All of my senses were heightened and my sense of knowing was at full peak. Information streamed into my body and a confidence that comes with full surrender was who I was.

Macchu Picchu was another park in the Disneyland of energy junky paradise. One morning, Ryan and I caught the early bus and ventured up the mountain to explore on our own. We took plenty of time alone at the gateway to the sun and giggled as we compared our perceptions of each area of the site. It was pure playful fun. I felt like a little kid, a little kid just full of joy.

The large group journey ended and a few of us continued on to Lake Titicaca at Puno and then further into Bolivia to the Islands of the Sun and the Moon.

The Island of the Sun is spectacular and Lake Titicaca is absolutely my favorite spot in this journey. The waters are magical, and once again, I could not resist the urge to immerse my body in them. As soon as our boat reached the dock on the far side of the Island of the Sun, I broke away on my own and headed for a pristine beach. Moments later, I was naked in the waters as they danced in electric sensation against my skin. The burn of the cold disappeared quickly as one recognized the magical qualities of the water. This beach and scene are embedded in my mind and comes up whenever I'm instructed to find my most favorite place in nature.

The journey to the lake is where dear friends from Bulgaria and I connected more deeply. Daniel and Silviya are an adventurous pair who has found a deep love through the bond of their spiritual connection, both coming into their second marriage. Owning and running a string of Italian restaurants in Bulgaria, they manage them by placing highly qualified people in charge of day-to-day operations, supporting them through Skype. This gives them the opportunity to travel the world and explore their intuitive callings while creating employment for hundreds of souls and serving delicious cuisine to their clients.

I have been the guest in Daniel's home for dinner many times since meeting them and it is a treat beyond imagination. This man has a gift for imagining ingredients and then being able to taste their combination in his mind. He is brilliant!

Silviya is a manifester with great power. She follows the impulse of her inner guidance and simply knows when she knows. They are a passionate and beautiful example of partnership.

One night over dinner on the Island of the Sun, they shared stories of their experiences drinking sacred plant medicine at a retreat center in Costa Rica. Indigenous shamans from Ecuador were brought to an ethno botanical sanctuary on the ocean to prepare and serve ayahuasca. In a ten-day ceremony, participants would go through cleansing rituals and sacred ceremony to experience the power and healing of the plant in the care of shaman steeped in the traditions of the medicine.

As we all listened to their story, my whole body received that resounding *"YES"* that tells you that you've already booked the flight.

For some time before, I had begun to hear the word ayahuasca in my dreams. It was just the word, and sometimes I would wake chanting it. Ayahuasca is a sacred plant found in South America. An exact combination of plants goes into the creation of ceremonial medicine, which has a hallucinogenic-like effect. This herbal mixture has been used in sacred ceremony for centuries.

Modern journeyers have ventured into the lands of the indigenous to experience its healing and educational qualities. The ritual and intention that goes into the creation of the brew is the most important aspect. It is vital that one pays close attention and feels into the energy of the people creating the medicine, and holding the space as you open to such a vulnerable experience. Taking personal responsibility for what one calls in is vital in every life experience, but here, it is critical.

I have never been one comfortable with anything that makes me feel out of control. I smoked a little pot when I was younger, which, initially, had pleasant effects of heightened sensual perception, but quickly moved to paranoia and the urge to get clean. I would smoke a little too much and then head for the shower in an attempt to wash away the feeling of being coated with the gunk of fear and shadow.

Sometimes, I would feel that sense of greater awarenesses and would often find myself writing down the most profound awakenings, but when morning arrived, none of them ever made any sense.

When Ayahuasca began to show up in my dreams, and then began to sound as a chant in my waking moments, I took notice with great curiosity. Once again, as though a greater power had come in to alleviate all fears and allow me to experience, the plant began to call me closer. Daniel and Silviya's stories were further proof.

One night in particular, I woke from a dream, and in this dream, I was standing in a jungle, peering out over sands toward an ocean. A man stood on the sand, staring into my eyes, and said, "Ayahuasca."

And I asked, "Who are you?"

He replied, "Jonathan."

I remembered his face very clearly and even made a note in my diary. Mostly because I wondered who the man was and why I felt such a connection to him.

As soon as I returned to Alberta from Peru, I booked my journey to the Costa Rica Retreat Center, and the next set of journeys began.

# Chapter 16

I drove from Alberta to Sedona in late November 2010, just two months after Peru. I visited with dear friends and then decided to spend a month in Kauai with my friend, Tiffany, the gifted sound healer I traveled to Egypt and France with and had stayed in Sedona with. She had moved to Kauai the spring before and was excited to have me visit.

Shortly after I arrived, ayahuasca was greeting me again. This time, I was given the opportunity to experience the medicine before I went to Costa Rica. I felt into the invitation and decided I would do it, fully giving myself permission to bail out at the last minute if I wanted. I would put no pressure on my mind for this. It had to be willing.

When the medicine, which had been brewed in South America, arrived in the house, I was curious to know how it felt. It seemed to be calling my name from the back of the fridge. Three days before we were set to experience it, I took the bottle out of the fridge, sat at the dining room table, and simple held it in my two palms. I could instantly feel dense, zigzagging vibrations flowing from the bottle and into my hands and up my arms. I was thoroughly impressed by the intensity of the sensation and wondered what this magical feeling was.

I felt completely enticed by the whole call of its unique, spirited quality. This was a living essence in my hands like nothing I had ever experienced before. I held the bottle for about fifteen minutes and then placed it back in the fridge.

That night, I was sick. I mean, coming out both ends sick. I couldn't figure it out. I didn't feel ill, but I was purging in a deep way, and when that process ended, I slept so deeply. I was completely oblivious to the fact that my roommate was experiencing the same thing, a few hours delayed.

I ended up continuing to cleanse by fasting the next couple of days and really being clear about what liquids and juices were coming into my body. I was unknowingly being prepared for the deeper ceremony that was coming. The medicine was clearing my physical body first.

On the day we were to drink the medicine, I took a beautiful swim in the ocean and pampered my restful body. I was excited and a little apprehensive, but assured my mind that, if for any reason it didn't feel right in the moment, I would not partake. It would be completely voluntary for my mind.

I spent the afternoon on the floor of my room, doing Yoga and writing out some intentions and prayers for the ceremony. One of the things that Silviya had shared about the medicine was that it was like a spirit all of its own, and that you could talk to it and ask it to be gentle with you. She said it had compassion, but to know that if it chose to take you somewhere, you would need to surrender or it would take you by force. It was going to be in control, not me.

Somehow knowing that Silviya and Daniel had done this gave me such peace and confidence that I could do it, too. They are such beautiful and gentle people with hearts of radiant light. How could this be harmful in any way when they are so pure in nature?

I wrote out my request for a gentle and educational experience, but most of all, I asked for it to be fun. I really wanted the experience to be fun.

Fun was my new mantra being in Kauai with all of the beautiful, playful *ohana*. I was completely in a blissful element of play as mother earth was nurturing me in her fertile and lush womb. Having been exposed to so much fire in all of the practices of Kundalini and the basic temperaments of the desert, I found that the water and earthy cradle of the island was healing me.

In fact, on my drive down to Arizona a month earlier, I found the energy in my body exploding upward at unexpected times. One of those was as I was driving through six lanes of traffic in Salt Lake City. The energy erupted and rose with much intensity, only to slam against my neck as though running into a brick wall. I'm sure it was because the reaction sent my head backward and I cut off the flow.

When the experience happened in Salt Lake, I pulled over and checked into a hotel. A short conversation with my teacher assured me that all was good and that a deeper conversation would be helpful once I arrived back in Sedona.

Once I arrived, Sraddhasagar wisely took me right into the garden and sat me on the earth. "Angela, you need water and earth. Go somewhere to ground and cool the fire."

Kauai was perfect.

The ceremony was about to begin and Tiffany knocked on my door to summon me. *Last chance to say no*, I said to my mind, but it was quiet and obedient like a child. There were three of us participating while Tiffany was to hold the space and lead us through the magic. Tiffany has a natural ability to connect in and align with the goddess frequencies. She is so beautiful and loving, and when she steps into the role of holding the container, one feels safe and nurtured.

She placed beautiful crystal goblets around the altar and brought out the medicine in an elegant decanter. She poured small portions of the liquid, which resembled molasses in consistency and color. We each held our cups and said a few loving prayers and intentions, and then brought the goblets closer to our lips.

I began to raise the cup to my lips, and before it actually touched, I could feel the energy jump from the glass ahead of the pour and enter my body. It made me giggle inside at the whole sensation of it meeting my body before the substance arrived. I thought, *"Maybe I'll just drink half."* Before I knew it, some outside force had emptied the whole thing down my throat. It was my hand that moved, but it was not my energy.

Within seconds, the whole left side of my throat and face began to tingle with rushes, but not the light, fluffy energetic rushes you get from energy moving. This was like a crawling, squiggly force of energy that was slippery and serpent-like moving through my tissues. Again, this brought a giggle for release. This stuff was working so fast that I was once again unsure if I had actually drank from the cup yet.

In a couple more seconds, the teeth on the upper left quadrant of my mouth began to feel as though they were disintegrating out of existence, and then a fright passed through me. Silviya's voice returned, reminding me that I could talk to the spirit of the medicine and ask for things. That was exactly what I did. I greeted the spirit with my internal voice and asked that it be gentle with me. I told it that I wanted to experience its teachings, but I did not want to be scared. My teeth immediately came back into the sensation of form and things slowed just a little.

Within seconds, the psychedelic lights of rainbow colors and prisms began to bounce from my eyelashes. I was dazzled and my attention shot off like a little kid chasing a shiny penny. Before me in the room appeared this beautiful, large feminine serpent. She was so colorful and iridescent in nature. She rose up and faced me square in my eyes, peering deep into my soul, as if to find the core of me and connect. We connected. She was huge!

Next, I felt her body enter the base of my spine and rise all the way up until she reached my head. As she entered my head, she bent her head forward to peer out of my third eye. I let go completely and surrendered my body like a puppet on an arm.

As though wearing my body as her suit, she began to stretch into the depths of me. It was the coolest sensation ever as I took a backseat to the ride.

Starting in my head, she moved side to side and then stretched deeply into the neck and shoulders. A couple of times, I wondered if I could truly stretch that far. Yet my body began to release deep-held contractions that I had never even connected with.

Once she had fully captured my head and neck, she worked my spine, bending me side to side and front to back. Each vertebra was moved to create length and space around it. This unlocked its mobility potential. I was being taken for a complete ride. No muscle in my body was activated. I was simply hanging from her like a beautiful garment.

Then the magic started. She began to move my body in circles. I was sitting cross-legged on the floor and she rotated my whole body from the base of my spine in circles. My spine was arching backward, moving the vertebrae as if they didn't exist in solid form. My head swept along the floor as she maneuvered me in ways I cannot duplicate.

Tiffany was holding this loving and amazing space of magic as she watched me with eyes fixed as this being fully took my body and interfaced with tissues, guiding me from her pure essence. Yes, the energy was female.

The journey continued as my heart began to burst open with deep knowing of divine, unconditional love for everything and everyone. I felt so full and cracked wide open. Other people in the room were having varying experiences.

One beautiful Buddhist goddess created mudras in the air and looked as though she was doing profound work for the whole universe. The other had been taken forcefully by the medicine and was purging all that no longer served her. She lay on the floor, gazing into my eyes with such radiance that we both joined in a state of awe. Even though her experience was rough, she was in a state of surrendered bliss.

Tiffany and I began singing from the depths of our love of life and we all shone like rays of the sun. My fingers ran through the strands of my hair as I marveled that they were pure light antennas gathering the juiciness of joy and bliss, and drawing it into my body. I carried this bliss of being weeks into the future, still in a heightened state of my connection to everything and everyone. The spirit of the vine was now within me and would be always. She was my teacher.

Once again this experience showed me that it's the mind that contracts and causes the body to take its form. When I let go of the mind and gave my body to the spirit, it was able to move me and shape me in any way it liked. Ways I cannot duplicate, all because my mind surrendered its hold on the body.

All of the Yogic training and metaphysical and scientific explorations pointed to this fact, that the mind creates the form, but now, I had an actual embodied experience to add to my collection of knowledge. This alone was so deeply profound that I would never forget the power and ability of the mind.

# Chapter 17

As the plane took off from Lihue, departing the island of paradise, I had to consciously release my feet from its soil. This was the beginning of tears I would shed each time I would leave a loving community. The *Ohana* in Kauai adopted me on sight and I felt at home in a nurturing space. The tears made me realize that I was longing for a deeper connection with community, and maybe even a home base. I promised myself I would be back the soonest I could.

Returning to Sedona after being in such a feminine, watery environment suddenly revealed the masculine intensity of the Red Rock Country. I knew it was always a place of deep transformation, but now I felt its strength and power in a different way.

Soon, I would be off to Florida for the winter solstice celebrations with the 3HO Kundalini crowd. There I would once again experience the White Tantra profound meditation practices. I was excited and I was tired. I had been moving nonstop all year, it seemed, and while that was profoundly life changing, it was also beginning to beg me for integration time.

The gathering in Florida for winter solstice was smaller and had a cozy holiday feel to it. This time, I set up a table in the bazaar and shared information about the pendants with all of the camp attendees. It was fun getting to know everyone, but most fun to be placed at a table beside Akal Sahai. He is a yogi, well known for his journey with bound lotus.

Bound lotus is a challenging practice where one sits in full lotus, legs crossed with feet resting up on the thighs. Once in this position, one bends forward and reaches his or her arms behind the back, grasping opposite toes with the hands. If I lost you in the description but you have the visual of a pretzel, you've got it.

In the practice, the yogi sits for fifteen and a half minutes in one configuration of the arms and legs, and then switches and does the opposite for another fifteen and a half minutes. During this time, one simply meditates, breathes, and lets all of the sensations pass through him or her. Can you imagine? As I write, Akal Sahai has done almost eight years of daily practice of this posture. Yes, I mean every day.

To sit and allow the densities and contractions within the body to dissipate, day after day after day, in this intense posture, one's form simply becomes hollow. That is exactly what it feels like when you hug Akal Sahai. He feels hollow. He is becoming purified in physical form, and as a result, pure spirit flows through him.

His personality is funny and he loves to watch you laugh. He is humble and thinks it's cool to experience everything. He is an absolute gift to the world and I am grateful to know him. He has written many books on "Being the Lighthouse" and resides in the eastern United States.

Akal Sahai is in demand as a partner for White Tantra because he is so clear and beautiful. I felt very humbled to be invited to be his partner the first day. I quickly agreed.

Once again, the rituals began and we sat fixed in our postures, completely glued in our connection for the whole day. I felt like I saw God in him. I am so grateful that we keep our connection.

It's actually funny because, when we phone one another, we invariable drift off into a silence and just sit in perfect stillness, within a field that spans thousands of miles across phone circuits. He completely holds a vast space for me and, like a perfect gentleman, waits for me to break the silence. Sometimes, that takes forty minutes or more. The energy of the field is so palpable, gently vibrating, and opening deeper perceptions. He's amazing.

Costa Rica was next on the itinerary. After flying back to Phoenix on Christmas morning, and spending the holidays in Sedona with friends, I hopped a plane and headed south.

I don't know what it is about flying near of over the equator, but I like it and I feel really good in the air. Once again, I was met at the airport and whisked away to a hotel for the night. San Jose was yet another new airport and city where I didn't speak the language.

Somehow, I managed to navigate using hand signals, and that becomes a fun game of charades. Mostly, I benefit from the fact that others have taken time to learn my language. I am so inspired by this that I have added learning Spanish to my list of things to do.

The next morning, our retreat group assembled at breakfast and we were taken to another airport for a short flight farther southwest. We were heading for a southern Peninsula. The whole journey was spectacular. The flight was followed by a boat ride up a river and then out onto the ocean, where we rounded the peninsulas and found our way to the beach near the center. Along the way, we saw alligators, serpents, and birds of such unusual markings. It felt so good to be in this moist and luscious environment.

The property we ventured to is an eco-retreat center founded by a man dedicated to preserving sacred medicinal plants and their traditions in ceremony. After living and learning in care of a group of Sequoia shaman in Ecuador, the proprietor had begun to bring groups to his oasis on the sea in Costa Rica to experience the magic and healing provided by such experiences.

After we arrived, we were shown to our rustic accommodations. Beautiful pathways filled with colorful foliage and flowers led us deeper into the property amongst the sacred trees. I was thrilled to find a dear girlfriend from my Peru journey already settled in the bunk beside mine. Here we were, together again to deepen our connection in a whole new land and process. Together with one more beautiful soul, we shared the space, which seemed to be nestled right in the trees.

Our meals were lovingly prepared from fresh vegetables and fish, all local ingredients. The whole center was predominately solar powered with a backup generator that ran a couple of hours each night. It was the perfect nest in which to incubate in the ceremonies. We gathered to meet our host and begin our time together.

His name is Jonathan, and, yes, he was the man from my dream. Chills poured through my body and a deep, profound knowing that I was exactly where I was supposed to be filled me. Why would I ever doubt any guidance? It was so clear!

The first three days, we woke at 3:00 a.m. to do a sunrise ceremony. The shaman created a concoction of weakened medicine, adding additional herbs beneficial in cleansing the body. We would drink the mixture from hollowed-out gourds until the tummy was so full that we could effortlessly expel it back out. Because we had no food in our bodies, it was like washing a pot rather than the unpleasantness of throwing up.

This was easy for me. The first Yoga teacher's training had prepared me through the *kunjal* practice of drinking salt water and expelling it back out. To cleanse the upper digestive organs this way not only clears the body of toxins but also allows one to release stuck emotions.

These three days were pretty easy for me and I settled in like I was back at 7 Centers in another Yoga training. The first of the initial three days brought rain that poured steadily on us throughout the entire ceremony. I was soaked to the bone despite rain gear but was fully surrendered, knowing that it was an additional purification and considered a very good sign.

Most of these first three days were like simple cleanses. Some days, I would feel the medicine and begin to experience the start of the spirit teachings. It was mild and I was getting very comfortable.

The shamans were like little magical beings, fully expressing children in little old man bodies. They were adorable. I could not speak their language and so could not talk directly with them, but that didn't seem to matter. Simply sitting in their space left one resonating in whole conversations that transpired in the stillness of

171

silence. I would always leave feeling more centered and with deeper knowledge of some aspect of my being.

The ceremonies were nothing like the bliss-out session I had experienced in Kauai. This time, the spirit would teach me lessons that required me to surrender further beyond the mind.

We would fast one day, drink the medicine that night, and then play the next day. This cycle would start over on the following day until we had drunk the medicine three times.

We began by bathing in waters filled with herbs and flowers. Our faces were painted with markings and designs. The first night Rodrigo, a younger shaman who accompanied the elders from Ecuador drew an apple tree on my forehead and giggled. I later learned that the apple tree symbolizes immortality, love, beauty, youth, and magic. That all sounded good to me! For the next two ceremonies, we were able to draw our own creations on our faces as we dressed for transformation.

We entered the sacred space after being smudged with sage and embraced by a beautiful goddess who assisted in the rituals. The medicine was carried from its place of creation along a pathway into the building, and we were asked not to cross that pathway until the ceremony ended the next morning. The path that the medicine took allowed the spirits to follow it, and crossing it would interfere with their journey, we were told.

As we entered, we were led to hammocks and mattresses to settle in for a night of journeying and the ceremonies began.

Soon, we were called up to receive the drink from the elders. All the while, they sang and sent prayers into the medicine. It was watery compared to the Kauai mixture and had a bit different taste, yet a familiarity that was unmistakable.

It took longer to take effect and my mind was starting to compare the experiences with judgment. That is the gift of experiencing something new. When you have no idea what to expect, there is no anticipation, just experience. When you've had an experience, the mind looks to duplicate it. My mind was going to be disappointed.

This first night, the medicine began by igniting a fire in the base of my spine that quickly roared with intense flames. Thank God for my *Vipassana* meditation training, as it enabled me to follow the sensations in the body with awareness. These were sensations that matched the most challenging of labor pains I had experienced when giving birth to my son. With all of my practices, I was able to just witness and not freak out.

The fire would race up the spine and slam into a block at the back my heart. The slam was hard against the blockage and then the sensation would relax a moment. Then in a sudden burst, it would do it again. This happened a few times, but I did not count. I just breathed.

Then, as though someone was standing behind me with a hot poker freshly retrieved from the fire, I felt it pierce through the back of my heart, shooting all the way through the front. The poker was streaming light into my body with such volume that it burst through me, splitting open seams of shining rays of light. The gasp of breath I retained was the full length of the whole experience. It was quick and short.

After that, a warm, lava-like feeling coursed through my spine like a river clearing deep between the crevices of my vertebra. This was soothing and calm. Smaller fires erupted randomly throughout the tissues and areas of my body. Each one would ignite a 3-D picture of the stored experience held in those tissues.

Some of the 3-D pictures had brought up the people involved in the story, and then conversations between us would ensue. We had resolved an issue or dilemma and then released it like a popped bubble of soap. It was good. I was being shown exactly how I had recorded my life right into my body. Things that blocked my flow and no longer served me were being revealed and transformed in the element of fire that the vine brought in.

I even had one conversation with my father where he explained that his radio connection to his body was fading out and that he couldn't get it tuned in. He was losing his connection to his body. He shared that this scared him and that he felt lost. In reality, there were days when he was losing clarity. He seemed to fade in and out at times, and the amount of sleep he had had played a significant role.

Other experiences during the weeklong event included studying the forces of expansion and contraction as my body was sent repeatedly through these journeys. The second night, my hammock was the one near the exit to the bathroom. Fellow journeyers continuously bumped against my hammock on their way out of the gate. They didn't mean to, but it happened, and each time, it would give my body the signal to contract.

At first, it annoyed me, but then I rode the wave of the action as it uprooted deeper and deeper contracted energies throughout the evening, as if it were a shovel digging deeper to extract toxins from my subconscious mind. Each contraction would bring it up and each expansion would let it go. The whole night was a continuous oscillation between these polarities.

I also watched the dance of the energetic layers of my body as they integrated with one another, and moved in and out of balance and alignment. I saw how the chakra field served to align them when it spun in balance and clarity. The medicine was teaching me all night.

The third night was all about my heart. I drank the medicine, but I felt blocked. The more I realized this, the tighter my body became. Had I become immune to the medicine or was I just done? I couldn't seem to go into the journey as the night began. I felt too clear and that the medicine must not be working. I drank more than usual that night.

Still, I felt little was happening and my mind was extra active. But then, I realized that I was watching angels step out of bodies, revealing the true nature of my friends. One in particular giggled at me as I caught him with fully spread wings in the room. I was comfortable in this reality and very lucid. I also knew that my medicine days were complete, at least for now.

The shamans were calling up people each night to do additional healings, but somehow, I got missed. I surrendered it and simply rocked back and forth in my hammock as I watched the sun rise and anticipated a beautiful breakfast. I couldn't help notice that I felt a sense of disappointment. Where was all the bliss of the

Kauai journey? Why was my heart so blocked? How could I leave this great experience feeling my heart blocked?

The group began to dissipate and return for showers and breakfast. I slowly made my way back to my room to shower and rest on my bed. I wrote in my journal a little and made my way down for the meal. One of the women on the journey was also the mother of young adults. She and I had a great visit, and in that moment, she asked me about my son and the next leg of my journey.

One of my nieces was getting married a couple of weeks down the road near Manuel Antonio on the Pacific side of the country. My son was flying in to join us. This woman's heart was so loving and open, listening to me intently, and before I knew it, I was in tears, sharing the pain I felt from when I had left my son and husband. I shared how guilty I had felt about having to leave my son. Even though he was grown, it affected him, and although we had been in continuous touch, things were awkward sometimes. Because that was painful, I was letting my guilt block my heart. I cried and cried, and all of my angelic friends beamed love at me, and embraced with hugs and looks of compassion.

I wandered back to the ceremony space to rock in my hammock and found the shaman still sitting with the medicine. I asked through a translator if it would be possible to receive my healing in that moment. I was set up on the wooden stool with my back to Raheleo, who seemed more serious than Tintin, the other elder. But he had a gentle energy, and as he worked, he was fully engaged in multiple dimensions.

He sang and shook a branch over my shoulders, back, and head, and I just sat, relaxed in the post-tears release that took my body. It must have been a half an hour or more that he sang. At first, I could only feel the block in my heart and wished for it to release. Hadn't that hot poker burned it free? And then I suddenly found myself realizing that the block was gone and I felt a vast space of peace. As soon as I consciously became aware of that, Raheleo stopped. I turned to thank him to find tears streaming down his face. Raheleo had cried all of the tears in my heart for me. I was left wide open and clean.

# Chapter 18

All of the journeys and practices of the past many years had enabled me to move beyond the limitations of my fearful contracted mind. I was now in my body and fully listening to the little voice that was actually my true self and not some outside force.

She was leading me all over the planet to experience different forms of healing and clearing, as knowledge was being awakened and embodied at a rapid and intensive pace. She took me over cliffs so that the mind could surrender to her charge. And finally, the obvious question was coming to mind. Why?

Why was I being led and cleared? Why was I jumping off psychological cliffs at every turn? What was the purpose of all of this?

No matter what I did, there was always the next piece, the next journey, the next practice, the next instruction from my little voice. I was on some kind of progressive quest to expand my awareness, but where was it leading? And what was driving it?

Initially, my intent was to fix myself, but we were beyond that now as the mind came to know its place as the autopilot of my form. The practice of observing what arises in the mind would be a lifelong practice. So if fixing myself wasn't the point, where was I going?

There I lay, in my hammock, completely relaxed. Hearing the birds and monkeys over the sound of ocean waves crashing against the beach. As the breath in my body expanded to fill my now peaceful heart space, I kept wondering where I was going.

Yes, I felt more comfortable in my body. I had come so far in my courage and I was no longer my mind. It was my tool. I rocked and swayed, inhaling all of the scents of the jungle, and my whole body began to tingle with rushes of energy that built with the sound of the breeze in the trees.

Getting in the body was just the first step. Cleansing its pathways so I could flow fully within them was merely avatar vehicle maintenance. All of this was just preparation for the next point of the journey.

We all come from formless, divine, unified consciousness. We travel through a body, learning the mechanics of creating with conscious awareness.

Here we are interfacing with a body and body-mind that is capable of honing and directing our frequency, the distillation of our thoughts, emotions and intentions, to literally manifest through a physical projection lens. Now that I had discovered this, what would be next?

The little voice began to teach me through an analogy. *"Look at the Internet,"* it said. A full understanding came easily into mind.

What is the Internet but a virtual electronic representation of the same thing that I was experiencing as I merged energetically with everything and everyone in my life? Circuits and pathways in my body and beyond were opening like links and coding through the Internet, merging and interfacing in depths of connection and communication. Wherever I placed my awareness I would connect, just like typing a web address in the Google search bar and hitting enter.

This was the next step! To follow the pathways and connect. To see that despite our illusory physical form, we are one mass of vibrating energy. One consciousness. One Heart. One breath. One being reflected in many faces. The mantra of "we are all one" was suddenly filled with meaning beyond the rhetoric of new-age speak.

That is why this journey of plant medicine was to clear my body and heart. That is why I was being shown grand states of bliss and full, energetic connection with the earth and other people.

What I had strived to suppress, in longing to belong within society, at any cost, may have been distorted because it came through a mind driven by fear and the illusion of separation, but the essence of this drive to belong came from the very fact that we are on a journey to merge with each other. To remember we are already connected. It is written right into the human DNA.

Longing to belong is the fuel that drives it all. Look at water. You can channel it down pathways and you can dam it up, but it always seeks to spread, flow, and merge with itself. We are the same. The body is merely a channel through which we pass. There is nothing to fear. There is only love and the re-mergence into this expanded awareness of being, of being fully unified.

The next leg of my journey would be all about connection. It was time to shift from a journey into my body to now expanding beyond it. What would follow would undoubtedly be perfect, as perfect as every moment of my life had already been. To look back, while swinging in that hammock, at every single experience, I saw a bigger purpose and flow to all of it.

Gratitude filled me and excitement rose as I wondered what bigger picture would be revealed as new puzzle pieces would be discovered.

This was just the beginning. There was no destination to arrive at. Nothing to fix. Next would be my expansion through the body. Next would be sharing the practices I'd been given. Next would be the divine union of our essences through sharing and merging in every possible way.

Next would be the waking and activation of the goddess energy, the sexual energy, the creative energy, to merge in the unified field of the divine. I was ready to merge in every way that was possible!

I would no longer run from the encounters of deep energetic connection for fear of blurring lines with sexual energy. I would explore it all. I would invite souls to meet me in the unified field to a depth that felt natural and right in the moment.

Whether it be sharing an idea, practice, emotion, or the intimate merging of bodies, I would strive to be naked and authentic in every meeting. I would continue to face the mind's limiting programs with neutrality and simply rewrite them. I would continuously learn to be more and more authentic.

In a few short years, I shifted from a woman of looping fears, who needed fourteen lists and two meetings for a journey to the nearest big city, to a global traveller jumping every psychological cliff in front of her. I knew nothing less than continuous transformation would do from now on.

As I swung in my hammock, I felt a sense of contentment knowing that the little voice would take me every step of the way. In those moments I didn't know what that looked like.

I didn't know that breathwork would become a powerful practice and offering. I didn't know that teaching Kundalini yoga and philosophy would inspire me to deeper practices of sexual healing and tantric arts. I didn't know that sharing my journey in a series of books was going to unfold.

I just knew that I was so grateful that I had been roused from a deep sleep within a mind that was confused about reality. I would go anywhere and do anything my soul longed for. This avatar form was both a sophisticated earth rover and an absolute gift. How grateful I felt for this life!

And so back to Sedona I went. *"It's time to wake the goddess,"* the little voice whispered. Whatever that meant.

# Afterword

T hank you for joining me as the little voice in my head led me on a journey of self-realization. From a woman filled with fear and contraction to a global traveller seeking the next psychological cliff to jump, I learned to literally get inside my body and be comfortable in my own skin.

From esoteric experiences of brain training, Kundalini activations, plant medicine, breath work, yoga, medical intuitive training, sexual healing and more, the complete *Body Ascension Series* shares a wide array of tools and techniques that bring true self into the body to interface with and express through our physical avatar forms.

Book One, *Avatar Anatomy,* was my journey into the body as I learned to recognize the guidance of my true divine self, following it blindly as it led me to open the energy pathways to fully embody my true essence. Once in the body, the realms of the subtle energetic world opened to my perceptions while notions of needing to fix myself fell by the wayside and a deeper understanding of truth and love was remembered.

Book Two, *Waking the Goddess,* is my exploration of the Shakti energy for connection and creation. The Shakti is the powerful creative and sexual energy that can be circulated within ones own body and shared with another. When honored in a sacred and conscious way, one may channel it toward positive healing and manifestation. This leg of my journey opens me to energetically merging with all souls to the depth and intensity called for in the moment. Whether through teaching a practice, sharing a conversation or merging intimately, I learn to get fully naked in my authenticity and expression by facing the ultimate fear of vulnerability, peeling more and more layers of limiting belief patterns away and inviting all those around me to do the same.

Book Three, *The New OS,* is my understanding of the times we are in. Beginning with downloads I received at the time of the 2012 shift in Sedona, AZ, I share the details of a whole new operating system for the mind, its process of unpacking and installing, and the inspiring forecast of what it means in where we are heading. Like crossing through the event horizon of a black hole, we are moving from a world of duality to a space of unity. I document the experience of my own mind as it grasps to understand its place in this new dimension, finding immense peace and unwavering faith.

Often people seek to raise the consciousness by moving beyond the body in the higher realms and frequencies. But in reality we are ascending within the body, bridging heaven and earth through the channels of our spines. *Body Ascension* explores the mechanics and implications of this amazing time we live in and seeks to inspire all souls to open their bodies and channel their true selves.

Thank you for exploring this lens. It is my deepest wish that you feel inspired to be all that you truly are. We each have our own path to ascension. I pray that you will enjoy walking the one that is yours.

*"May the long time sun shine upon you, all love surround you, and the pure light within you, guide your way on." ~ Incredible String Band*

Sat Nam and Love,
Angela

For more information about Angela's Writings and Body Ascension Playshop Offerings, visit
www.bodyascension.com or www.angeladitch.com

Made in the USA
Charleston, SC
28 March 2014